This book is dedicated to all those who came before us
and those who stand beside us in spirit.

Frontispiece & Cover by Amanda Manesis

DEEPER INTO THE UNDERWORLD

DEATH

ANCESTORS

AND

MAGICAL

RITES

CHRIS ALLAUN

Copyright © Christopher Allaun 2018, 2022

All rights reserved. No reproduction, copy or transmission of this publication may be made without written permission. No paragraph of this publication may be reproduced, copied or transmitted without permission or in accordance with the provision of the copyright act of 1956 (as amended).

Cover art/design Amanda Manesis www.amaradulcis.com

Other works by Chris Allaun
Underworld: Shamanism, Myth, and Magick vol I
Upperworld: Shamanism and Magick of the Celestial Realms

Contents

Introduction 7

    Deeper into the Underworld we go…; The Underworld; Astral Projection and Shamanic Journeying; Astral Exercise #1 ; Astral Exercise #2 ; Astral Exercise #3 ; Exercise: Finding an Underworld Guide and Spirit Animal ; Finding Your Spirit Animal; Finding your Underworld Guide.

1 Death 22

    Coyote and the Origin of Death (Caddo Native American); Death; Our Fear of Death; Angel of Death; Azrael Goes to Mother Earth; The Creation of Death (Hindu); The Death of Yama (Hindu); The Energetic and Physical Process of Dying; What Happens to the Energy Bodies After Death; The Karma and Destiny of Death; Judgment; Exercise: Remembering Death ; Facing Your Own Death; Exercise: Writing Your Eulogy; Exercise: Your Own Funeral;

2 Ancient Ancestral Practices 52

    Orpheus' Search for Eurydice (Greco-Roman); Ancient Pagan Worship; Necromancy; Ancient Egyptian Death Rites; Embalming; "Opening of the Mouth"; Book of the Dead; Greco-Roman Temples of the Dead; The Path; The Kidnapping of Persephone; Rites of Eleusis; Exercise: Meditation of the Ear of Grain and Regeneration; The Ghost Dance; Exercise: Dancing With the Ancestors; Exercise: Ancestor Dance Ritual.

3 Honoring Our Ancestors 79

    Those Who Come From The Mountain (Japan/ Shinto); Modern Pagan Honoring of the Dead; Building an Altar; Honoring and Devotion ; How the Dead Appear; Evolution and Transformation of the Dead; Dreams with the Dead; Ancestor Dream Ritual; Exercise: Meditation on Being an Ancestor ; Meditation: Trickster Spirits and Negative Entities ; Finding an Ancestral Teacher ; To

Find Your Ancestral Teacher: Astral Traveling to Experience the Ancestors ; Traveling to the Ancestors to Release Ancestral Patterns ; Family Karma ; Performing Tasks for Ancestors ; Magick with Ancestors ; Calling Ancestors in Ritual.

4 Necromancy 121

Baldur's Dreams (Norse) ; Necromancy ; Reasons for Summoning the Dead ; Sacred Places ; Sacred Times ; Cemeteries ; Mausoleums; Tombs and Mounds ; Graveyard Meditation ; The Hidden Company ; The Rose Castle ; Ritual of the Rose Castle ; Summoning Spirits of the Dead ; Ritual Outline ; The Dead and Cursing ; Healing and Removing Curses ; Forcing the Dead Against Their Will ; Re-Animation; The Sorrow of Isis (Egyptian) ; Fears of Re-Animation; Asclepius and Diana Bring Back the Dead (Greco-Roman); My Thoughts on Modern Re-animation.

5 Skulls, Bones, and Blood; Odin Enchants Mimir's Head (Norse);

The Skull; The Skull Meditation; Initiation of the Bones (Skeleton Meditation); Gravestones; Oracles and Guides; Blood Magick; The Blood of Creation (Maya) ; Witchblood; Hyndla and Freya (Norse); Tapping into the Blood; Exercise: Tapping into the Blood; Journeying To The Blood; Blood in Magick and Necromancy ; Mayan Ancestral Blood Summoning Ritual ; Spellcasting Using Blood.

6 Magical Protection 191

Talking to the Spirit; The Broom or Besom; Blast of Power; Wards; Banishing Without Prejudice; Laughing; The Magical Ring;Herbs/Crystals/Stones;Chemicals; Incense and Fumigations; Ancestor Magick; God Magick; Talismans/Charms/Medicine Bags; Mirrors; Ritual to Banish Unwanted Spirits or Demons ; Valediction.

Other Works 207

Bibliography 209

Index 215

Introduction

Deeper into the Underworld we go…
We celebrate the cycles of life, growth, and renewal and connect ourselves to the flow of nature. But what of death? Death is a natural part of the rhythm of life and rebirth. There is an ebb and flow to all things. Everything that is created must end and be dissolved back into the energies of the Universe. Death is as sacred as life. It is because of our mortality that we strive to be more than we are and find happiness and fulfillment in our lives. It is believed that the oldest rituals in human history are death rites. These are the ceremonies that help the dead transition to a place of healing and peace in the Underworld. In our modern magical practice, it is important that we incorporate the ancient practice of honoring Ancestors and magick. In our modern culture, we send our Ancestors to the afterlife in the Underworld and then forget about them. It is time we bring them back and honor the beloved dead just as we honor nature and the gods.

There are ancient secrets kept in deep in the Underworld. It is said, "The dead tell no tales…", but they do. To those who know how to speak and honor the dead, they can tell us their tales. The dead have secrets of the life they lived and energies of death, the afterlife, and other magical rites. They can add power to our magick and tell of coming events. In my previous book, *Underworld: Shamanism, Myth, and Magick* we learned about the subterranean world. This is the world of our ancestors, those souls who came before us. It is also a place of healing and dreaded creatures who are diligently kept out of our reach. As we have learned, there is much power and wisdom to be obtained in this magical place. But there is much more to explore. We must go deeper into the Underworld and discover who our ancestors are and how to bring them into our world so we can help each other through magick. We honor the gods and spirits of nature around us, but we are missing a vital part of our spiritual development. By honoring our ancestors, we are connecting with the powers of the Underworld in a balanced and healing way. I am a firm believer that to spiritually evolve, it is beneficial to connect to the gods in the Upperworld, the spirits of nature in the Midworld, and the Ancestors in the Underworld.

Our Ancestors are our family and loved ones who have come before us and, through death, passed beyond the veil that separates the physical world and the spirit world. Our Ancestors do not necessarily have to be of our family lineage. They can be friends or people from a particular creed, association, and magical lineage. It is through our bloodlines that the more common concept of "Ancestor" comes. The same blood that runs through your veins also ran through the veins of these Ancestors. The DNA in our blood and bodies comes from both mother and father. I feel that it is important to note that different cultures stress the value of lineage through one parent more than the other. Some cultures feel the father's blood and heritage has more value, while others place more value on the mother's blood and heritage. I think both are important! To pick one over the other is to deny half of who you are and half of the potential magical power you could achieve.

When it comes to bloodlines and heritage, it is important to know your family history so that you can better assess which talents are predominantly found in which side of the family. For instance, if your mother and grandmother were natural healers then it will be in your best interest to work with that side of the family for natural healing. If, at the same time, your father's side were craftsmen, then it will be best for you to work with your father's family for that type of magick. Sometimes, we are unaware of the magick that runs in our family. If we use craftsmen as an example, such as metal-working or blacksmithing, there are many ancient traditions that believed that the craftsmen who created the sword or the plow blade held a lot of magical power. As you go forward on the journey of learning about our Ancestors, you may discover the magick that is rooted deep within your own family history. Remember, to do magick several centuries ago was illegal and therefore was hidden, sometimes even from one's own family.

The Ancestors are not only found in our genetic DNA of our biological parents. They can also be found in our magical groups and spiritual traditions we follow. This is what we call a magical lineage. As the same blood runs through us as it did our Ancestors, so does the magical current run from the beloved dead of our spiritual traditions down to us. I have many students who do not know who their biological ancestors are or have decided not to include their family on the ancestral altar. Instead, they chose to honor their spiritual family instead. I have seen many wonderful ancestral altars who honor founders and teachers of their tradition instead of their grandparents and relatives.

It is important to know where you came from and who your Ancestors are, but this, sometimes, is not as easy as one might think. If a person is adopted or there is no record of parents and grandparents, then I think it is perfectly valid to learn about the Ancestors from those people you call family. Ancestors are more than who gave birth to you. It is about who you are and where you come from. It is about those spirits of the dead who are willing and able to connect with you on a profound spiritual level. As we have seen, groups and creeds can be the Ancestors that you link up to. With this being the case, there is nothing wrong with using your adoptive parents or stepparents in your workings. I have seen on occasion when someone works with the Ancestors of their adoptive parents that, after a time, one from their biological family makes themselves known. But I will caution that this is not always the case. Sometimes the gods and spirits have decided to sever that ancestral cord for whatever reason. Remember that the gods have your best interest at heart, and they know more about destiny and the cosmic web than you do. Learn to feel the love of whomever you call Ancestor and take heed of their guidance and advice. You might be surprised just how powerful they can be.

I have been working with the ancestors and the dead for many years now. I cannot imagine a world where I do not speak with my family in the world of spirit. Not only have they aided in my magick and spiritual journey, but they have done many things for me that I could never repay. On my ancestral altar, I have a space for my grandparents and great grandparents. They protect my home and keep the energies balanced and conducive to healing and magick. They are my family in spirit just as they were my family in life.

The Underworld

The Underworld is a place that is home to the ancestral afterlife as well as other concepts that are found in myth and legend. There are numerous pagan spiritualities that place the beloved ancestors in an energetic or spiritual place beneath the earth. Such a place is called by many names by various cultures. The Egyptians call it the Dwat, the Greeks call it Hades, the Nordics call it Hel, the Welsh call it Annwn, and so forth. The ancestral lands are wonderful places of healing, rejuvenation, and spiritual learning. But the Underworld has dark places as well. When Zeus conquered the Titans, who caused chaos upon the earth, he bound them deep into a horrible place called Tartarus. And then there are the hellworlds and shadowlands that lost souls are said to be doomed to wander.

In pagan and some indigenous cosmology, the Underworld is but one of the shamanic three worlds that is symbolized as a giant tree that makes up the Universe. The trunk of this great energetic tree we call the Midworld, or sometimes the Otherworld, it is the place of humans, faeries, elves, plant and animal spirits, and the spirits of the land. The great branches which reach into the heavens is the Upperworld. This is the place of gods, angels, planetary and star spirits, and ascended beings who guide the spiritual evolution of the Universe. Then we have the roots of the tree which travel deep within the earth itself. This is the place of the ancestors, the wandering dead, chthonic deities, and even sometimes demons. Together these three worlds make up the energetic or astral Universe that we can journey through in spirit. Each of these worlds has wonderous beings who can teach you magick and healing. For us, in this book, we will work with the ancestors and the dead so that we may find healing and the deep mysteries of death and the afterlife.

As we journey deeper into the Underworld you will discover your ancestors, ancestor teachers, and spirit guides who will teach you of the mysteries of the Underworld and the dead. These powerful beings are waiting for you to call upon them and establish a deep and meaningful relationship. Your ancestors have been waiting for you all this time. They have been watching you and waiting for the moment that you will use your magick to summon them in your rites. That time is now. Welcome to the deeper parts of the Underworld.

Astral Projection and Shamanic Journeying
To travel into the Underworld, you will be using your astral body. The astral body is our energetic double and is sometimes called our body of

light. The astral body can be easily controlled by the emotions and the mind. When you become proficient at leaving your body, which is called astral projection, you will have the ability to journey through time and space. You will be able to travel at the speed of thought to anywhere in the Universe.

I have studied a lot of books and been to workshops that teach astral projection. When I was a novice magician, I remember learning the formulas and magical invocations that would allow me to leave the body in spirit. The magical spells seemed exceptionally long and the techniques for leaving the body were tedious and it took months of meditation and visualization exercises to even get one's feet wet. To most students, this was daunting and left people feeling more frustrated than empowered. After receiving a formal magical training followed by a lot of experience traveling to the three shamanic worlds, I can tell you that you that astral projection is very simple - you just have to practice at it with some regularly and not get discouraged if you do not immediately get results. I will give you a couple of fun exercises to do that will get you started. The key here is to visualize as clearly as possible and *FEEL* the sensations of walking around, seeing, hearing, smelling, and touching. To do this you simply use your imagination. Visualize. The other key to controlling your astral body is to use logic, imagination, desire, and will. Meaning, you must imagine yourself in the Otherworlds as clearly as possible using logic, then with the desire to travel, you simply will yourself to do so.

The first few times you may wonder if astral projection is just "all in your head." Well, to some extent it is, but it is supposed to be. Remember, the Astral and Spiritual realms are the places of imagination, dreams, and visions. We travel around in the physical plane in our physical bodies, so we travel around in the Astral/Spiritual with our astral (imagined/visualized) bodies. I know some magicians who will argue with me that I am oversimplifying ancient magick. And I am. If at first it feels like it is "all in your head" go with it. Eventually, you will meet entities, spirits, and gods who will take you to wonderful places and tell you secret information that you simply cannot "make up." The trick here is to have fun and explore. See what you find. Read some of the mythology listed in Suggestions for Further Reading at the end of this chapter and try your best to understand the spiritual meaning behind the stories. Then go have a spiritual adventure.

So, what is all this talk about shamanic journeying? Basically, shamanic journeying and astral projection are the same thing. You are using your astral or energy body to leave your physical body to travel in the spiritual realms of the Universe. The term "astral projection" is more popular in ceremonial magical and New Age communities while "shamanic journeying" is a term more popular in neo-shamanism. At the end of the day it really does not matter what term you use because the end result will be the same.

Astral Exercise #1

1. It may be helpful to play a shamanic drumming recording. If you have someone to drum for you all the better. The drumming should be light but audible enough to hear comfortably. If you are using a drum or having someone drum for you, have them beat at a moderately quick pace. If for some reason you cannot get a recording of shamanic drumming, don't worry. It is not necessary to have a shamanic drum beat to astral project. If you do not like shamanic drumming feel free to use any type of music that puts you in a trance and makes you feel magical. I will often use synthesized songs that sound ethereal to accomplish this for myself.

2. Sit or lie in a comfortable position. Make sure your back is as

straight as possible.

3. Close your eyes and take a few deep breaths.

4. Relax your body as best you can. Begin with your feet. Tell them to relax and release all tension. Then move up to your calves. Tell them to relax and release all tension. Go up to the thigh, glutes, back, belly, chest, shoulders, arms, hands, neck, and head in turn, telling them all to relax and release all stress and tension.

5. Imagine yourself getting up and walking around. Remember, this is done entirely with your imagination. Try not to move your physical body at all.

6. Walk around the room you are in and look at the furniture, walls, shelves. Look at yourself. See yourself lying (or sitting) down.

7. When you are ready, see yourself walk over to your physical body and sit or lie back into yourself. When you are close to your body this will most often happen automatically.

Astral Exercise #2

1. Play your shamanic drumming recording or other music as per the previous exercise.

2. Sit or lie in a comfortable position. Make sure your back is as straight as possible.

3. Close your eyes and take a few deep breaths.

4. Relax your body as best you can. Begin with your feet. Tell them to relax and release all tension. Then move up to your calves. Tell them to relax and release all tension. Go up to the thigh, glutes, back, belly, chest, shoulders, arms, hands, neck, and head in turn,

telling them all to relax and release all stress and tension.

5. Imagine yourself getting up and walking around. Remember, this is done entirely with your imagination. Try not to move your physical body at all.

6. At this point, see a door or gateway in front of you. Know that the door leads to the World Tree.

7. Step through the door and on the other side see the World Tree. The Word Tree is the largest tree you have ever seen. Its trunk extends out further than the eye can see going both left and right. The branches go up into the heavens and you cannot see the top of the tree. You can see that the roots go deep into the Earth.

8. This is the Center of the Midworld, and it is your starting point. Until you are very proficient with traveling, you may want to start here.

9. You notice that there is a door in the trunk of the tree leading down, deep into the roots of the tree. Go through the door. You may see a staircase or simply a tunnel.

    Note: You may also simply see a hole in the ground leading down into the Earth, following the roots, leading down into tunnels.

10. Go down further and further into the roots through the tunnel or staircase. Know that you can travel down very fast and sometimes in just a blink of an eye.

11. Finally, when you arrive at the Underworld, take note of the first thing you see. Explore the immediate environments carefully. When you are ready, go back the way you came and back up the tunnels into the World Tree, then back to the trunk of the tree and into the Middleworld.

Astral Exercise #3

1. Play your shamanic drumming recording or other music per the previous exercises.

2. Sit or lie in a comfortable position. Make sure your back is as straight as possible.

3. Close your eyes and take a few deep breaths.

4. Relax your body as best you can. Begin with your feet. Tell them to relax and release all tension. Then move up to your calves. Tell them to relax and release all tension. Go up to the thigh, glutes, back, belly, chest, shoulders, arms, hands, neck, and head in turn, telling them all to relax and release all stress and tension.

5. Visualize a spiral of light, beginning at your feet, spiraling around you, going clockwise. It surrounds your entire body. The only thing you can see is the spiral of light. Know that this magical spiral of light is transporting you to the World Tree.

6. This is the center of the Midworld, your starting point. Until you are very proficient with traveling, you always want to start here.

7. You notice that there is a door in the trunk of the tree leading down deep into the roots of the tree. Go through the door. You may see a staircase or simply a tunnel.

    Note: You may also simply see a hole in the ground leading down into the Earth, following the roots, leading down into tunnels.

8. Go down further and further into the roots through the tunnel, or staircase. Know that you can travel down very fast and sometimes in just a blink of an eye.

9. Finally, when you arrive at the Underworld take note of the first

thing you see. Explore your immediate environs carefully. When you are ready, go back the way you came and back up the tunnels into the World Tree then back to the trunk of the tree in the Middleworld.

10. After awakening from your journey, record your experience in your magical journal and ground yourself back to the physical plane. You may do this by eating something light, drinking water, and/or doing "everyday" things around your home.

At this point in learning about astral travel and journeying through the Underworld, it is not about trying to see how far you go or finding exotic places right away. It is about taking the first steps in learning a new skill. Just as with any skill, it takes practice. You must remember, the astral body is a direct manifestation of your mind, desires, memories, will, and your imagination. What this means is your astral body looks like how you want it to, does what you want it to, and looks like what you think it will. Usually, the astral body looks like you do now but in more "idealized form. Therefore, if you look at your astral body in a mirror, you may look younger, stronger, and healthier.

The astral realm itself takes on the appearance provided by your mind, or the group mind. As we have stated before, if there is a locked gate or a blocked entrance way, most likely your subconscious mind has put it there because either you are not ready to go forward in that direction, or you *think* you are not ready because of your own personal fears. When this happens, try to find out why you cannot go through, or come back later. Group mind phenomenon happens in the Astral/Underworld when we discover ancient sites such as Hades or Hel and they look exactly like the ancients described them. This is because of the many people who believe it looks a certain way. This massive thought form echoes through the astral and takes form. The more people who believe something to be true, the stronger it manifests. This is the reason why each Underworld of every culture around the world exists. This is also the reason why there is no "one truth".

Exercise:
Finding an Underworld Guide and Spirit Animal

In order to successfully journey into the Underworld, it is important to find your Spirit Animal and Underworld guide. You will be able to explore the Underworld faster and find treasures and allies much quicker than you would if you traveled alone. Also, the Spirit Animal can protect you from dangers that you are not ready to face. Your Spirit Animal can also protect you from spirit attacks in the Underworld. Spirit attacks upon a beginner are extremely rare, and I have often found that the "attackers" are really projections of the traveler's own fears. Put simply, the beginning student is "attacking" him or herself in the Underworld because of their own fears. In essence, they believe the Underworld is a dangerous place, so they imagine danger at every corner. This is simply not the case. The Underworld does have some dangerous places, but the world of the Ancestors is a place of beauty and spiritual transformation. However, your Spirit Animal can help you fend off this astral thought form, should it occur.

Finding Your Spirit Animal
For this exercise, you will travel to the Midworld to find your Spirit Animal.

1. Choose one of the astral exercises from the section on "How to Use Your Astral Body" above and travel to the World Tree.

2. Once there, make the following statement: "I wish to find my Spirit Animal". Open your heart chakra and reach out with your energies to your Spirit Animal. You may not know what kind of animal it is.

That's ok. Reach out with your heart and they will respond back to you.

3. Begin walking in whichever direction feels appropriate to you. Keep the goal of finding your Spirit Animal n mind and try to intuit the direction you should go. The landscape will vary from person to person. You may find yourself traveling into a forest, mountains, valleys, or grass plains. Trust your instincts. For the time being, do not worry if you are "making it up." Visualize your surroundings to the best of your abilities.

4. Keep an eye out for any animals you see. You may see several. Some traditions say that you may see other animals, but you will see your Spirit Animal four times as you walk along your path. This is a good approach to take.

5. If you do not see any animals at first, keep walking. You should eventually begin to see more and more animals.

6. Once you see your Spirit four times along your path, walk up to itand ask, "Are you my Spirit Animal?"

7. If the animal seems distant, unfamiliar, or unwilling to speak with you, then this may not be your Spirit Animal. If it is not your Spirit Animal, keep searching.

8. If the animal is your Spirit Animal, then it will feel like a long-lost friend or relative. Your Spirit Animal may even feel like a part of you. This is because in reality, your totem IS a part of you.

9. Ask your Spirit Animal its name and record it in your magical diary or journal upon returning to your physical body.

Once you are fully conscious, visualize your spirit animal in front of you. You may choose to dance with them or simply imagine your Spirit

Animal combining with your aura. To combine the Spirit Animal with your aura, visualize your animal in front of you. See them walking toward you and energetically combining itself with your aura. Know that you can call upon your Spirit Animal at any time in any world! I recommend getting an animal fetish - a little statue of clay or stone that represents your animal. If you have the fur, teeth, or a claw of the animal then all the better. These things are not necessary but do help you connect to them in a deeper way.

Finding your Underworld Guide

1. Choose one of the astral exercises and travel to the World Tree.
2. Once there, make the following statement: "I wish to find my Underworld Guide".
3. Call upon your Spirit Animal.
4. In the trunk of the World Tree, visualize a door that leads down into the Underworld. Follow this path down.
5. Follow this path down until you reach the Underworld. What do you see? What does the landscape look like?
6. Keep the intention to find your Underworld Guide in your mind. Begin to explore the Underworld. Ask your Spirit animal to show you the way.
7. Trust your intuition. Look for people along the way and ask them if they are your Underworld Guide. If not, ask them to point out the direction in which you can find your guide.
8. Once you find an entity who is a likely candidate to become your Underworld Guide, ask if they are willing to help you navigate the Underworld. If the answer is "no," the entity is not your guide, and

you should keep looking. If the answer is "yes," ask for their name. Then ask your guide if there is anything they would like in return. If the request is reasonable and you are able and willing to do it, then by all means do it. If not, graciously explain why you cannot meet the request.

9. Know that you can call upon your Underworld Guide each time you enter the Underworld.

10. Come back to the Middleworld the way you came. Then open your eyes and journal about your experiences.

The Underworld is a wonderful place to find transformation of the spirit. It is through the myths that ancient cultures have learned to navigate and find their way through the strange terrain. The power of the Underworld has many great rewards for us and to the community we serve. As we learn how to use our astral bodies, we will begin to further our understanding of the world that holds a vast amount of wonder and beauty. Take some time and discover what the Underworld has in store for you. Journal your experiences and the beings you encounter. Write down what happened and the names of the spirits and gods that you meet. Each day you will develop and strengthen your relationships with the Underworld beings, ancestors, guides, and many other spirits who will help and guide you upon your spiritual path.

1
Death

Coyote and the Origin of Death
(Caddo Native American)

In the beginning of the world, there was no death and the people lived forever. Soon, there were so many people that no one knew quite what to do! Food was running out and it began to get very crowded upon Mother Earth. All the chiefs got together to decide what to do about this dilemma. One chief explained that people should die for a little while then come back. He explained that if people died forever then their families would be very unhappy and everyone upon the Earth would be sad.

Coyote objected! "If people only died for a little while," he explained, "then eventually it would still be crowded and there would not be enough food for everyone!"

The chiefs did not listen to Coyote. They decided that people would die for only a while. Then they would bring them back by building a grass lodge and singing a special medicine song. They would summon the dead to the grass lodge and restore them back to life!

Soon the time came to bring the dead back to life. The grass lodge was built and then the special medicine song was sung. A spirit of the dead in the form of a whirlwind came up to the lodge. But Coyote couldn't stand it! He knew the world would be overcrowded and the food would run out. In a flash, Coyote slammed the door to the grass lodge and the whirlwind passed by the lodge. This is how Coyote made death eternal.

Death

The ultimate mystery has always been death. Death takes our loved ones away from us. Death seems final. When we are told about death at a young age, we are told the spirit of our loved one has gone to Heaven, or someplace nice. As we grow older, we begin to seek the answers of death ourselves. We ask ourselves and the Universe questions, such as, "Is there life after death?", "Is there Heaven and Hell?", "Will I exist after I die?", and "Will I have a consciousness after my mind dies?" All these questions are valid and have been asked by every single person at least once in their lifetime. We turn to religion, priests, and spiritualists to find the answers that we seek. We hope that someone has the truth…or at least some part of it. Most of us were born into one religion or another. For a moment, it seems comforting that our parents and the members of our community believe and "know" that there is a heaven or some other kind of salvation at the end of our lives. We take their word for it, hoping that the people who came before us know what they are talking about. When we close our eyes and fall asleep, we dream. Is this similar to life after death? But what about those moments during sleep when we do not dream, or we do not remember our dreams? Is that oblivion?

Humans have fantasized, written, made plays and movies about, and feared death more than anything else in this world. Death is the finality of our existence in this time and space on the physical plane. It is frightening and it can be macabre. It is the end, at least, of how we perceive things from the point of view of our lives here and now. For if there is life after death everything will be different. Even if life after death is almost the same as it was in life, one thing has changed…you have died to the life you know now.

When we look at art and movies about death we see the tragic loss, pain and suffering, sorrow, and the frightening personification of death.

Nothing about death seems soft, beautiful, and happy. In most of the patriarchal religions you either follow the word of God and are blessed at death with angels escorting you to a place next to God, or you do not follow the word of God and you are damned at death with demons dragging you down to be tormented for all eternity! No wonder so many people fear death. It may ease your mind to know that this view of death is relatively new in the history of religious worldviews. The ancients did not believe in a permanent place of torment for even the most wicked of souls. Some, however, did believe in a place for lost souls, or a place for lost *parts* of your soul. But they did not believe in the gods' punishment for not adhering to rituals and scriptures. Tribal villages most definitely did not believe in such a thing. Nor did they believe in "sin" as we understand it from a Judeo-Christian perspective. The idea of sin and the punishment for sin was never found in ancient times. If we take this into account for our own view of the Universe and the cosmos, we begin to see more possibilities. We will begin to see that there is more to the energetic Universe and the three worlds than we once thought. It opens new ideas and perhaps experiences that we never thought could be possible.

For some, death can be beautiful. They can see God in the process of decomposition of the body. The process of decay is a part of the universal cycle of birth, death, and re-birth. All things that are created thrive and then must be broken down or destroyed for the cycle to continue. Even our own solar system was, in theory, born from the death of a previous star. This is the way of things. We know from our teachings that nature abhors a vacuum and does not waste. Waste is a human behavior. Nothing goes to waste in the Universe. When a star dies, its gases and energies are used by gravity to create new stars and planets. When animals (including humans) die, or produce waste, it can be used to give nutrients to plants and our crops. Through this process the cycles of life, death, and renewal we can continue. These cycles are what allow life and magick to continue. If we see death as a part of the Universe and a part of the cycles, then it can be a beautiful process. There is beauty in all things, even decay.

When we begin to experience the world on our own, we learn that, perhaps, our parents and religious leaders may not have all the answers. The truth is that NO ONE has all the answers. Yes, that is correct. NO ONE. Not even those with a vast knowledge of Spirit. What I mean by this is that no one, no matter how wise and powerful they are has the entire truth and all the answers of the afterlife. It is true that each of these people have experiences that they can share with us. We must remember that these experiences are *their* experiences and may or may not have a direct impact on us. We also must remember that as holy people and magicians explore the Universe, the Underworld, and communicate with the dead, that their experiences are colored by their hopes and fears, prejudices, and worldviews. This does not make them wrong; this makes them messengers of their experience. It is important for you to have your own personal experiences and come up with conclusions for yourself. Mythology, lore, and the experiences of others are a good starting point, but it does not end there. If we look around, the world and the Universe are evolving and changing. Nothing stays the same and cycles go forward and become something greater than they are now. We must continue our own personal explorations and find new experiences. As we work with the dead and the Underworld, we will never come up with the whole truth. Various cultures have distinct ways of thinking and relating to the world. Therefore, we need to be aware that different peoples and cultures have a variety of ideas and experiences.

Perhaps in the end, we are looking at the same thing but just explaining it differently.

Our Fear of Death

Humanity has feared death from as far back as anyone can remember. Part of the fear of death comes from our built-in instinct for survival. To not have this instinct would ensure that early man would prematurely go to their deaths like antelope jumping off a cliff; fear of death makes you move quickly in the opposite direction when you notice a large predator coming your way. Many religions speak of salvation or of being in a "better place," but for those who are unsure or do not believe in religious teachings, death can be a frightening thing. It is even worse for those who believe that they have lived against religious teachings and are convinced that upon death they will spend eternity suffering.

It is interesting to note that there are numerous types of fears that people have when it comes to death. Some people fear dying without a will. Others fear the pain of the death process. But what about when people think you are dead when you actually are not dead! Before modern times there was a fear about being buried alive. There are many conditions that mimic death. There are conditions where your breathing and heart rate slow dramatically and you appear dead. It fascinates me to know that there have been instances where a grave has been dug up only to find that the inside of the coffin was torn up from the inside. Some might say it was a Vampire, but we know it was a person who was mistakenly placed in the grave. Unfortunately, this did happen from time to time. This was one of the reasons for having the custom of the wake. The idea was to put the body on display to see if the person would "wake up." Nowadays, with sophisticated medical equipment, we no longer have to worry about being placed in a coffin without actually being dead.

There is also the fear of the body and the tomb being defiled. There were, and still are, grave robbers. These are people who dig up graves to steal jewelry or expensive mementoes that may have been placed in the coffin with the deceased. Grave robbers have little consideration for the dead and their philosophy is "they won't need it." I think this is horrible. In my worldview, whatever you place in the tomb or in remembrance of the dead belongs to them and they have access to the item in the Afterlife.

An interesting, and to my way of thinking valid, fear of magical people, is the fear of their body being used for Necromancy and black magick after death. For most people, magick does not exist and this would be an irrational fear. But to those of us who believe in magick and the power of energy, it is something that is very real. The Greeks and Romans have many stories of dark magicians who dug up and stole a corpse to summon the soul of the dead out of Hades and use them for divination and cursing. The ancient Celts were headhunters and sometimes used the skulls of their enemies as an oracle. It is from Africa that we get the concept of a zombie, actually gaining control of a dead body to get it to cause harm to others. In reality the "zombie" is an unfortunate person who has been exposed to a dark magician's blowfish powder, which causes nerve and brain damage, and it is much easier to control a susceptible person under the influence of the powder. For people who are concerned about dark magicians using their body parts, it is always wise to have strict orders to be carried out by the living concerning what to do with your body at death. My best recommendation would be cremation. However, do not allow people to keep any of your ashes. Have them spread out somewhere. Your ashes can be used to summon your spirit from the Underworld.

There is also the fear of feeling the process of decay in the grave. In our modern times bodies are filled with embalming fluid, which keeps the body preserved longer. On a scientific level, the brain dies soon after the body and it would be impossible to feel the process of decay because the nerves would all be dead. However, on a spiritual level there is the fear of the spirit lingering in the grave and being unable to pass on to the next world. I have personally never come across a spirit to whom this has happened. The Underworld spirits and gods would not allow that to occur. In my opinion, that would upset the cosmic balance of things. Plus, there would be no spiritual purpose or lesson for the person in question.

Lastly, there is the fear of being forgotten or not living up to your potential during life. I think that it is our spiritual programming for us to carry out our destiny during life. We are put here in the physical plane to learn, evolve, and heal each other. Each of us has a special destiny and reason to be here. Some people find that reason very quickly and others take a little longer to find out their life's purpose. Unfortunately, there are those who never do. The fear of being forgotten is a very real thing. The best advice I can give you on this subject is to evaluate your talents, get advice from teachers and mentors, and meditate on your will and spirit. If you ask the Universe for guidance, it has been my experience that it will answer.

To fear death is natural. To not fear death in some way is to be sometimes reckless with yourself and others. We are all here for a reason and our goal is to carry out our destinies to the best of our abilities, not to rampage heedlessly through life without giving a thought to either the past or the future.

Angel of Death

The Angel of Death has been spoken of in Christian, Islamic, and Jewish traditions. He is commonly portrayed as a skeletal figure wearing a black hooded robe and holding a scythe. He is portrayed that way because he is thought to reap the souls of the living from Earth and bring them to the world of the dead. His appearance is nightmarish and his gaze sparks fear in the eyes of all living beings. You may see this figure at Halloween, and he is a character one wants to avoid.

In Jewish mythology his name is Azrael, which means "The help of God" or "Help of the One." In some myths, he was created after most of the angels because after the Universe was created, it was discovered that there must be an ending to all things so that they could begin anew. Azrael, the Angel of Death, was brought into being to carry out this purpose. Otherwise, the Universe would be overrun by living corporeal beings and the cosmos would be brought out of balance. He does not kill living beings or decide how they will die. He is sort of a psychopomp in the way that he takes the souls after death and delivers them where they need to be. In the Christian and Jewish traditions, it is thought that he takes them to either Heaven or Hell. In the modern New Age philosophies, he simply takes the souls to the Realm of the Dead.

When one encounters Death, or hears the tales of him, he is almost always portrayed as the shadowy silent figure that brings about death and fear without remorse. He is even portrayed as "evil." This is only superstitious belief brought about by fear. Azrael is not evil. He carries out a very sacred duty of the Universe. He brings balance to the cycle of life, death, and rebirth. When he is depicted in art, he is dark and has no "eyes," which is why he is sometimes thought to be cruel and soulless. In fact, Death appears to the living as we think he would look. In the psychology of spiritual phenomena, spirits and energies always take the form of how we expect them to appear. I, myself, have seen Azrael on several occasions and he does not appear to me as the gruesome character as he is depicted to be in art and movies. He has appeared to me in different ways, but generally he is the same in each of his visits. I see him dressed in a dark or black robe and he does have "flesh". But yes, I saw him as a pale man with jet black hair and dark eyes. He has never spoken to me directly, but communicates with energetic sensations, symbols, and emotions.

In my research on Azrael, I have found that he rarely speaks to someone directly. Commonly, the living can easily intuit what he is saying or seem to *just understand* what is going on. I believe this is one of the reasons that he brings fear to us. He does not communicate in the way we are used to. All angels have a specialized function, just as we ourselves have a special talent or skill. The Angel of Death does not enjoy the pain and suffering of living beings upon their death. He brings about the *release* of suffering. He takes away the pain of illness, accident, and mortal injury. In this regard, we can view him as an angel with great sympathy and someone who wishes to ease our pain and suffering. In healing, sometimes the way to ease suffering and pain is death. We must remember that Azrael is an angel, and it is not up to us to completely understand the mysterious ways of the divine or the Universe. Some things may not be meant to be understood but will always remain part of the mysteries.

In art, books, stage, and film, there have been depictions of love affairs with Death. To most people this may seem like one of the strangest things to do. There have been stories about the great passionate love affairs between women and men with the Angel of Death. If you think about it, humanity has always had a love/hate relationship with the entities involved with the death process. One reason for the love affairs, I believe, is the classic attraction to dark and shadowy men (or in this case, beings.) People are often sexually and romantically attracted to dark and mysterious men for many different reasons. Often, we want to learn about our own dark sides. Another reason for these love affairs with Death is because throughout history right up to the present being "in love" with a higher being is simply another form of devotion or even worship. To those who are not familiar with the pagan religions, this may sound a bit odd to be in love with a god, angel, or higher being. Many mythologies talk about how gods fall in love with mortals and mortals in love with gods. Think back to how the mortal Psyche fell in love with the god Cupid. It is important to realize that the myths about Death are no different. It has been said that we fall in love with those who help us evolve and grow in one way or another, and Death always plays a powerful part in our spiritual evolution.

There have been tales and theories that Azrael is one of the fallen angels. This is not true to the mythology of the Judeo-Christian angels. It is true that some of the fallen angels may cause sickness, injury, and death, but Azrael has no part in this. He is also portrayed as a dark and shadowy figure, but he is not a demon; nor is he a malicious entity. His position and powers make him a follower of the plan of God, and he stays true to his divine purpose. He never goes astray. I believe that the myths and stories that link him to the fallen angels were written out of fear and ignorance as to who and what the Angel of Death is.

So, the question is, in our work and exploration with the Underworld, do we summon, work with, or give honor to the Angel of Death? In Jewish practice you do not worship or honor the angels. You simply respect them as the messengers of God and listen to their guidance. In magick, there is the fear that if you summon Azrael then he will perform the duty that he was created to do, namely take your soul. I have never actually heard of a magick conjuration going that way. In my personal practice I do give honor to the Angel of Death in my own way, but I do not command his presence in any way. I give honor to the energies of Death and should Azrael have something to tell me then, well, I listen.

It is interesting to theorize about the powers of Azrael. Essentially, everything in the Universe must end or "die." Does the Angel of Death have powers over those things as well? Does he have power over dying planets, stars, and even whole galaxies? When our Universe returns to the place of origin and the Universe as we think of it now ends, will Azrael be there to carry the pieces back to God? These are all interesting concepts, and many theological and philosophical conversations can be had on this topic alone. But if it is true, and Azrael will be a part of this event, then truly he is the "Help of God", and God whispers things in his ear that only He and Death may know.

I had first met Azrael in a dream when I was 15 years old. I dreamed that I was babysitting three infants and they were asleep in my bedroom. My friends had pulled up to my driveway in a black van and wanted me to go with them somewhere. In the dream, I had forgotten about watching the infants and decided to go with my friends. As we were driving away, I could see a pale man with long black hair wearing a black robe in my bedroom where the babies were. He was spreading his arms wide open to show me his power and that he had captured the infants. Frantically, I dashed out of the van and ran into the house. When I got to the bedroom, the babies had their legs chopped off and Azrael was nowhere to be found. But I knew where he was! I quickly ran out of the house and found the van in the middle of the yard. The van door was open, and I saw someone with long black hair sitting in the back. I was convinced it was the Angel of Death. I found a screwdriver in my hand and stabbed the longhaired person who then melted away. I had beaten death.

When I awoke, I had the darkest feeling. Death had been there that night. I walked into the kitchen to make some breakfast when I heard my parents talking. They told me that my brother's best friend had a girlfriend who was murdered the night before. When I had my dream. My dad showed me a picture of her; someone I had never met before. When I saw the picture, my heart fell out of my chest. That was the girl I had stabbed with the screwdriver in my dream.

Another time I had seen Death was a few months after my father died. I was in bed listening to trance-like music. The candles were lit and there was a magical hue in the bedroom. My mind was aimlessly wandering. A dark presence appeared in my room. It was not clear, but it was like the primal earth of decay and endings entered my bedroom. I knew instantly it was Death. When Death appears in front of you, you do not have to guess. His energy is unmistakable. I had no fear of him because he was not there for me. He opened his cloak, and he revealed my father to me. Neither my father nor Death spoke a word. My father's eyes were happy and bright, and it was as if he wanted to see me one more time. After a moment of energetically connecting with my father, Death closed his cloak and slowly disappeared. I knew that Death did not do favors for people easily and there would be work that Death would later ask me to do.

Azrael Goes to Mother Earth

Yahweh sent the angels Michael, Ariel, and Gabriel to the Earth to collect clay so that he could create mankind. The three great angels flew down to Earth to do as God had asked. As they began to try to pierce the Earth, their angelic tools did not work. Again and again, they tried to dig into the Earth, but their efforts were useless. The three great angels had magnificent strength given to them by Yahweh himself. This made no sense to them! Why could they not obtain the Earth that they wanted? Yahweh wanted to create man and the Earth was impenetrable. How could this be?

They argued among themselves why Yahweh would send them down to creation to do an impossible task. They suddenly became aware that the Earth was alive with a consciousness of its own. The Earth was alive! Michael, Gabriel, and Ariel found Mother Earth. She was divine in her own right but was different than Yahweh and the angels themselves. They petitioned her for her clay so that God could create man. Mother Earth had the power of foresight. She knew that Yahweh's creation, the human race, would procreate and with the passing of time, man would destroy her. She sent them away. Their power was no match for hers.

Michael, Gabriel, and Ariel returned to the heavenly realm. They explained to Yahweh what had happened. There would be no clay. Yahweh then sent the angel Azrael down to speak with Mother Earth. The great Mother knew why Azrael had come, and again she refused to give him the clay for Yahweh. Azrael had great compassion for Mother Earth and her beauty. He spoke with her at great length about his divine powers. He explained to her that man would indeed procreate, but they would not live forever, they would be mortal, and he would take them in death. Mother Earth was comforted by his great compassion for her and the mankind that Yahweh would create. She agreed to give him the clay he had come for.

Azrael returned to the heavenly realms with the clay for Yahweh to create mankind. Yahweh was impressed with the compassion Azrael had for Mother Earth and his ability to take away that which he had created. Yahweh made Azrael the Angel of Death. It is Azrael who holds your hand for the journey into the great mystery.

The Creation of Death (Hindu)

In the beginning, humans did not die. They were multiplying very rapidly and were overpopulating the Earth. Brahma, the Creator, was concerned about this so he created the goddess of death, Mrityu. Mrityu was given the ability of great compassion. She loved all beings of the cosmos. Brahma told Mrityu of her most sacred duty…to kill all living beings at their appointed time. This greatly saddened Mrityu and in her grief she ran far away from the beautiful things that Brahma had created. Brahma pursued her, looking throughout creation to find the goddess. At last, when he found her, he explained her sacred cosmic duty and how the spirit of living beings would live on after death on the wheel of rebirth and would return to Earth in another incarnation. After understanding that the beautiful beings would live on in spirit, Mrityu agreed to be the goddess of death.

The Death of Yama (Hindu)

Yama was the first man that lived on Earth. There were no other people on the Earth except for his sister Yami. Yami wanted to have children, but Yama refused because he was horrified at the thought of having sex, much less children, with this own sister! Yami persisted, but time and time again Yama refused. When the day came, Yama died a childless man. Upon death, Yama entered the Underworld. As a result of being the first man to live on Earth and die on Earth, he was the first being to enter the Underworld. Unfortunately, he had no children that would have children so that he could be reborn on Earth. He was doomed to spend eternity in the Underworld. But the gods gave him a most holy duty. Since he was the first man to know death, he would be transformed into the Master, or God, of death! Ever since, when someone is doomed to die, it is Yama who takes him to the Underworld.

The Energetic and Physical Process of Dying

When we have come to the point in our journey on the physical plane that we must move on to the spirit world, the dying process will begin.

There are several things that are happening at once. The chakras have a direct effect on the physical body. What happens to the chakras inevitably happens to the body. As we know through our magical and spiritual studies, things manifest first in the astral/energetic planes before they manifest on the physical plane. The same rules apply to the process of dying. We have seven major chakras that correspond to the seven major parts of the body.

1. Root - sacrum, pelvis (Earth)
2. Navel – lower back, bladder, reproductive organs (water)
3. Solar Plexus - midback, upper abdomen, spleen, liver (fire)
4. Heart - heart, lungs, chest, thoracic (air)
5. Throat - throat, cervical, thyroid (spirit/sound)
6. Brow - midbrain, eyes, sinuses in skull (spirit/sight)
7. Crown - cranium (spirit/divinity)

During the death process the energy of our chakras dissolves. Our physical body and our chakras are connected and what happens to one happens to the other. When the chakras no longer have the strength to help our body function, our bodies stop working. From an energetic point of view, our chakras quite literally hold our body's functions together. When we are dying, we are beings of matter returning to the world of spirit. The first chakra to stop working is the Naval Chakra. This is because it is where we hold our life force that connects us simultaneously to the physical world and the energetic world at the same time. Our life force flows to the naval chakra at birth and flows out of the naval chakra at death.

The order of how the chakras die is as follows:

1. Navel (water)
2. Heart (Air)
3. Solar Plexus (fire)

4. Throat (Sound)
5. Root (Earth)
6. Brow (sight)
7. Crown (spirit)

Earth dissolves into Water

The first thing that happens during the process of death is that the Naval Chakra begins to "dissolve." What is happening is that the Naval Chakra is returning to the energy world. By doing this there is a disconnect between the root and solar plexus chakras. We may feel heavy and lethargic. We may lose control of our bodily functions. In our minds, our perceptions will dim. You may feel spiritual "emptiness" and have delusions.

Water dissolves into Fire

It is here that the Heart Chakra begins to dissolve and the solar plexus unravels with it. With both the heart and naval chakras gone, the solar plexus cannot sustain itself without the support of the others. Your body will dehydrate, and you will feel like you cannot get enough water. Your mind will further become cloudy. Energetically, you may see a mist all around you.

Fire dissolves into Air

At this point, the Throat Chakra dissolves and the heat from our bodies is escaping through our breath. The fires from our solar plexus chakra have nowhere to go and this chakra has disintegrated and cannot control the warmth in the body. We may feel warm at first, then we will gradually become very cold. Our minds will be clear one moment then foggy the next from the fluctuation. Energetically, you may see sparks of light all around you.

Air dissolves into Consciousness

It is here that our Root Chakra dissolves and the air in our bodies become unstable. The root chakra keeps all of our body functions grounded and maintained in our physical body. Without this chakra, our body functions and energies deteriorate more rapidly. Our breathing will increase and then decrease. Our eyes may roll up into the back of our heads and our breathing will stop. It is at this point that we lose consciousness and will begin to hallucinate. What we hallucinate will depend upon our Karma. What we have done in life or more specifically, what we feel we did not learn when we had the opportunity will fill our minds. These mental projections will color our experiences in the Afterlife.

Consciousness dissolves into Spirit

Finally, our physical bodies have clinically died. Our consciousness, the ideas of self and ego, are taken out of our bodies and into the spirit world. It is from here that the subconscious projects karmas, emotions, hopes, and our fears and is manifested by the spirit world. It is here that the Buddhist "final thought" is transmitted for the spirits and entities to see. The final thought is the last thing you think about at the point of death. This becomes an astral thought form that colors how you interpret the Otherworld. This information will help or inhibit the dead in their travels in the Otherworld.

What Happens to the Energy Bodies After Death

As we have learned, the energy bodies are connected to the physical body. What happens to the physical body affects the energy bodies and in turn, what happens to the energy bodies affects the physical body. For example, when someone is cremated, there energy bodies are cremated. When a person dies, what normally happens is that the etheric, astral, mental, and spiritual bodies are separated from the physical body. After separation, the rest of the energy bodies remain intact for a time. Just as there is the natural function of decay for the physical body, the energy bodies will disintegrate and be absorbed back into their respective plane. The physical body returns to the Earth, the etheric body to the etheric plane, the astral the astral plane, the mental the mental plane, and the spirit remains on the spiritual plane.

The etheric body is the first to be detached. This normally happens soon after death. It simply disintegrates and is absorbed back into the etheric plane. When this happens, the deceased may freely travel the astral plane and wait for ancestors and spirit helpers to show them to the other side. I have heard some spiritualists say that there is an energy cord that must be disconnected from the body and the energy bodies. I personally have never seen this cord. Most likely this is because it is dissolved during the dying process. Sometimes, when there is unfinished business, the spirit of the deceased may not want to move on and desperately holds on to the physical plane. When this happens, the deceased may often appear to the living as a ghost. He or she may be unable, or unwilling, to move on until the business is resolved. This may range from solving the mystery of who killed them to watching over loved ones until they can take care of themselves. Each situation is unique and should be treated as such.

After some time has passed, the astral body is ready to be shed. The amount of time is left up to the individual and the circumstances surrounding the person's death. There is a faint connection between the physical body and the astral body. There are times when there is a lot of emotional baggage or anger, and the astral body may take on a life of its own. Because of all the emotional energy, the spirit of the dead may unintentionally create an "artificial elemental" with its own astral body. The astral body may then haunt a home or area that the deceased once felt strongly about. This happens on occasion. When the spirit of the deceased has moved on to the spiritual plane, it is no longer feeding the astral body with energy. The astral body may seek energy wherever it can, thus becoming a sort of vampiric entity. These entities must be destroyed, otherwise they may prey upon the living for their life force. There are also the rare times that a person's astral body may be possessed by a negative and destructive spirit or demon. Once this happens, the demon has access to all the memories, thought processes, and desires the deceased once had in life. This negative spirit may then use this knowledge to convince the living that they are the spirit of their loved one. It may go even further to convince the living family members to give the astral entity energy and offerings to keep it functioning in the physical plane. After all, to the living, it seems to be their deceased loved one in need of help from the other side. These spirits may manipulate the grieving for their selfish purposes. This is one of the various reasons why it is important for funeral rites to be performed. The magick that is performed at these rites helps prevent these things from happening. Cremation also prevents the astral body from being used for ill purposes. A dark magician may have the power to capture the astral body of the deceased to use in black magick. In some magical traditions, the magician can find and capture the astral body and store it in a bottle. I believe that this where we get the idea of capturing someone's soul in a bottle. Because the discarded astral body has little memory of consciousness and spirit of its own, the will is weak and can be manipulated. These situations are rare, but they do happen.

After the astral body has been shed, the mental body and spiritual body remain. Like the previous energy bodies, the mental body will be shed, and the spirit will return to the spiritual plane. The spiritual body is indestructible, but it can transform into pure spirit.

The Karma and Destiny of Death

In many spiritual communities, there is a belief in Karma and Destiny. The word *Karma* is Sanskrit for "action". Karma does not mean, "what goes around, comes around," or "an eye for an eye." These thoughts are a misunderstanding of the spiritual principles of Karma. Most of the people who believe in the "what goes around comes around" philosophy come from a Western background and are used to a spiritual system of rewards and punishments. This philosophy works well for people who need to be told what is right from wrong. The rest of us, however, are able to believe in a spiritual system that moves beyond these black and white concepts. Life is not black and white, and neither is the spiritual Universe. I have also heard of the Lords of Karma. In my research and understanding of Buddhism, Hinduism, and other studies, I have not found any such entity to exist. This is not to say that they do not, just that they cannot be found in any traditional teachings.

Karma is energy that the Universe gives people, plants, animals, and the entire cosmos for the purpose of evolution and transformation. The energies of Karma are there to teach us how to evolve into higher spiritual beings. When we fail or go against the divine flow of creation, then the energies of the Universe puts experiences in place so that we may learn from our mistakes. What sometimes happens is that the more often we make the same mistake the harder the energies become. This is because the Universe is trying to get our attention so that we may learn the lesson that is intended for us. Again, this is not a punishment. The Universe does not make bad things happen to us like a spiritual spanking! On the other hand, when we are going with the flow of the Universe and learning to become observant of our world and the lessons that are provided for us, then the energies seem to work in our favor. Think of the flow of the universal energies like the flow of a river. If we swim against the current, our lives seem difficult. If we swim with the current, then our work is much easier. To do this effectively, we must find out Divine Will, or life purpose, and keep steady on our spiritual path. By doing this, you will be going with the tides of power and spirit.

There are times when the Universe puts rocks in our metaphorical river. This is a lesson that we need to learn. I will admit that sometimes these lessons are very hard and very painful, and we do not think that we will get through them. And yet we do. A lesson such as this helps us understand who we are. It pushes us further than we would ever push ourselves. I will say, as a spiritual leader, the Universe has pushed me way beyond what I thought I was able to do. The lessons that were provided for me helped me understand the meaning of the universal energies to become a stronger magician, a more powerful healer, and to understand the human condition far better than I thought I was able to. The further you explore your spiritual path, the more the Universe will work to make you better than you are now.

Karma has a direct influence on death, how we die, and what happens to us after we die. Once again, I want you to understand that Karma is not a punishment. If you fail to learn your lessons, it is not taken out on you at the time of death. There are several thoughts relating to the topic of what role Karma plays at death. There is a theory that says that our death is pre-ordained by the Universe and the gods which points to a specific time and date. Another theory says that the time of death depends on how well you learned your lessons during life. If you learned every lesson quickly, then you may die quicker. If you are a slow learner, then perhaps you will live longer. If you believe this theory, do not try to "cheat" death by purposely not seeking to transform yourself spiritually. You are who you are, and you will learn your lessons accordingly, whether you like it or not; most likely such an action would just result in having the same lesson thrust upon you painfully time and again until death itself may be seen as a welcome release. There is also the theory that if you fall off your path dramatically you will die much faster than anticipated. Drug addicts, those with psychoses, and people who give up on life may fall into this category. This last idea says that death is dependent on spiritual lessons, how you live your life, and how well you physically take care of yourself and the world around you. I personally like this last theory the best.

Judgment

In our Western culture, the biggest fear of death is not the pain of dying, but rather the fear of judgment. Judeo-Christian cosmology teaches that if one does not live a life according to the will of God, or that laid out in the rules of the Bible, then God will place "judgment" upon you, which more often than not means that you will spend eternity experiencing the torments of Hell. The power of the Christian church came in part through its emphasizing that they alone, as the spokespeople for Jesus Christ's redemption and forgiveness, held the panacea for the pain and agony that would last forever and ever. In this way, the Church kept a tight control over their followers. The threat of excommunication meant that if you displeased the church, they could banish you from the grace and forgiveness of God. By doing this, you would go to Hell without delay upon dying. As we have discussed earlier, the Great Spirit that created all things does not punish. The Hell that the Christians speak of is of their own creation. Julian of Norwich was a nun during the 14th Century who had a vision of God and the afterlife. In her vision, God showed Julian that there is no Hell. She tells us, "Yet in all this I wanted (as far as I dared) to get a real sight of hell and purgatory…but for all of my desire I saw absolutely nothing…"

In my travels to the Underworld, the people who find themselves in a Christian place of punishment have put themselves in those places because they believe in the torments that are described for them by Christian priests and believe that they "deserve" to be there.

The Egyptians had a judgment process that may have inspired this way of thinking. Upon death, after the soul found its way through the Underworld, its heart was weighed against the feather of Ma'at. Ma'at means *truth*. There was a list of wrong doings that the person professed *not to do*. It was the wrong doings that made the heart of the spirit become heavy. If the heart was lighter than the feather of Ma'at then the spirit was free to dwell in the heavens with the gods; if not, then the spirit was given to the great monster, a creature that was part crocodile, part lion, and part hippopotamus named Ammit. Ammit then devoured the spirit. I do not believe that the spirit was destroyed, per se. But simply through being "devoured" by the monster, the soul was returned to the cycle of reincarnation and reborn on Earth to try to transform and evolve so that the next time they found their way to the scales of Ma'at they would fare better.

Other cultures also focused on the doing of good deeds as a prerequisite to getting into a good Afterlife. The Hindu version of judgment is Karma and the Cycle of Samsara, or reincarnation. If the spirit of the person held to Dharma, the adherence to their social role in society and devotion to the gods, then they might escape the cycle of reincarnation to be placed within the world of the gods. If not, they would remain in the Underworld in the land of the ancestors to await the proper time to be reborn. Interestingly, in order to be reborn, they might have to wait until their family members conceived a child. If not, the ancestors would become a ghosts and hunt the younger generation through dreams and visions to make them want to have children. Even when a person ascended to heaven, they could be cast down if they did not continue to do good deeds and carry out devotion to the gods in the Afterlife. In this cosmology, there is no Hell, only lower planes of existence that helped the spirit face their weaknesses in order to elevate into the higher planes of spirit.

In Nordic myths, the place of your afterlife depended on honor and your deeds on the battlefield itself. If a warrior was killed in battle, then they would dwell in either Freya's hall, Sessrumnir, or within Odin's great hall in the Upperworld, named Valhalla—the Hall of the Slain. Valhalla was a warrior paradise where every day one would engage in battle, then at night eat and drink until they had their fill. Men feared dying a "straw death," meaning they feared dying of simple sickness or old age. If this were the case, then the spirits of the dead would dwell in the Underworld in a world called Helheim. This was a place of fog according to some accounts, or, in others, a place that was eternally autumn. Spirits here had a less dramatic and exciting existence. Helheim is where Christianity get their word for "hell", but to the Nordics, it is a place of the Ancestors.

If we look closely at myths, the act of judgment is not to decide who is better or who is worse, or who failed at life or who succeeded. There is a much larger spiritual matrix involved that is much greater than our human minds can understand. It is about the great and wondrous spiritual Universe that is created to aid in our spiritual transformation. Some of the patriarchal religions are designed to assume that people are nothing but mindless primates who need the notion of good or bad, satisfactory or unsatisfactory, in order to perform right action. But these same ideas are set up in such a way that they punish the people that God created, simply because, according to Western Christian theology, they were created as flawed and sinful beings. I want to be very clear that in life, to make mistakes and to fail is how we learn. Those who do not make mistakes or feel the pain of loss and despair never go further in their development. If you think about it, if everything is fine in your life, what would push you to do greater things? It is only by failing that we grow. I am not saying that we should not be responsible with our lives or with the lives of others. What I am saying is that in the great cosmic scheme of things, the gods want us to do well. They help us in every way they can. But, after all that is said and done, ultimately the choices we make in life are our own.

Exercise:
Remembering Death

Everyone has had a family member or friend die. This is not something we can, nor should, escape from. Our thoughts and feelings about death can color our personalities and how we view life. We cannot fully appreciate the joys of life if we have not truly tried to understand our own feelings of death. In this exercise, we will explore our own feelings about death through journaling. Journaling about our memories of the past helps us remember the facts as we saw them. It helps us to stimulate emotions that we have long forgotten about.

I have found that it is helpful to keep a magical journal. This way I can write down my magical thoughts and experiences that I have so I can go back and reread them in the future. I have several so I use a simple spiral notebook. Take out your magical journal. Begin to write about everyone who has died in your life who was important to you, be it family, friends, classmates, or co-workers. Try to remember the facts surrounding their death and how you felt about them. This may bring up painful memories that you would rather not deal with. Good. It is extremely important that you understand, recognize, and, if possible, deal with any unresolved feelings about your loved ones' deaths. As we are working with death, the ancestors, and other spirits of the dead, it is important to understand how you feel with these energies. When you are working with the dead you do not want to be caught off guard with any unresolved or hidden feelings. Write down every little detail, thought, emotion, or anything at all that seems relevant. Do not edit yourself. This journal exercise is for you and for your spiritual development only. You do not have to share this journal entry with anyone unless you would like to do so.

When writing in your journal, try to remember every detail about how you felt when you heard the news of the loved one's death. You may have been in shock, sorrow, denial, or numbness. Write about the funeral or memorial service and how you felt before, during, and after the service. If there was not a funeral or memorial, how did you feel about that? Write about how the death of the loved one has had an impact on your life and your worldview. Did it change who you are? Finally, write about how you feel about the death of the loved one now. Are any of those previous feelings resolved? Are any of the previous feelings the same? If any of your feelings about the death has changed, write how they have changed. Write about any lessons you have learned because of the death. Do this exercise for each important person in your life who has died. The important thing to do here is to be very honest with yourself. Do not diminish any of the experiences.

One of the reasons we do this exercise is because in your work with the Ancestors and spirits of the dead, you may have a loved one come visit you for various reasons. They may visit you because they know you are doing this type of work or because they need your help in some way. You may also decide to place symbols of your loved ones on your ancestral altar. When an Ancestor appears before you with requests for important work, it will not help them or yourself if you have an emotional breakdown. However, you should deal with any emotions that should come up with this type of work. Another reason that it is important to do this exercise is because the more powerful you become as a witch, magician, or deathwalker, the more powerful the beings are that will take notice of you. Some beings do wish you harm and the best way to defeat an enemy is by exploiting their weaknesses. Spirits are masters at shapeshifting. A negative spirit may wish to weaken you by causing an emotional breakdown by appearing as your dead spouse, parent, or other loved one who passed through the veil. It is important to understand and deal with your emotions with death the best way you can so that you are not caught off guard. If you are having trouble with this exercise, it is wise to seek the advice of someone who is a trained professional counsellor who understands this type of work.

Facing Your Own Death

To work with the energies of the Underworld and with the Ancestors, it is important to face your own death and understand your fears pertaining to death and the afterlife. Most people do not fear the pain of dying or the transition into death. Most people fear oblivion. This is the idea that once your body dies and you are brain dead there is nothing else, only unconsciousness and darkness that you cannot perceive. You are gone. Everything you have learned is gone. Every great deed, every bad thing you have ever done is gone. Those memories of your family and friends are gone. The bonds that you created with your spouse are gone. You are no-thing.

The other fear many people, who were raised in the Christian faith, may have about death is that the Christian Hell really exists and that is where they are going when they die. In their minds, they fear the idea of an eternity of being in the Lake of Fire and feeling the agonizing pain of their bodies burning forever and ever as demons torture them.

Another thing that people may fear about death is the great mystery of what death really is. People have heard religious priests and leaders describe their version of what happens after death and the rewards of living a virtuous life and the punishments of living a shameful life. But the great mystery is that no one really knows what the Afterlife is. What if it is more wonderful than they say it is? What if it if far more horrible than anyone could possibly imagine? The great mystery itself is the fear and not so much what happens after you get there.

If you are a serious student of the Underworld and the Ancestors then you most likely do not have the fears listed above, however you may still have some concerns. There are many fears about death. Just as many fears, perhaps, as there are people. Everyone has their own hopes and fears of what is to come once their body and brain has stopped functioning. "What if" can be a truly terrifying mental exercise in certain circumstances.

While we are alive, we can never truly understand what the Ancestors have gone through, and we can only grasp as much as our limited understanding allows us. As we journey through the Underworlds, we must try to understand our own personal fears about death and try to relieve those fears the best we can. We may never truly conquer all of our fears about death, but we must learn what they are and perhaps where they come from so that these fears do not hinder us in the work ahead of us.

Exercise: Writing Your Eulogy

In this exercise, you will be writing your own eulogy. This will be presented when you have a mock funeral for yourself. When you write the eulogy, write everything that you would like someone to say about you as if you were actually dead and the speaker was reviewing your life. Write about all your achievements and the people in your life that you love. Write funny anecdotes and anything else you can think of to say. Later, the eulogy will be presented by someone who will preside over your mock funeral, or you may speak it aloud in a recording device to be played back.

Exercise: Your Own Funeral

For this exercise you will be giving yourself a mock funeral. The point here is to understand death in all of its stages. This stage is the funeral. Some spirits will linger around long enough to listen to their own funerals and memorial services. This helps them finalize in their minds that they are dead and will help them let go of the physical plane so that they may move on to the Afterlife. In Buddhism, it is believed that the deceased can hear everything that is said to and around the body. This exercise will help you understand what the spirits of the dead must go through. It will also help you deal with your own mortality on a more profound level. I will caution you that intense feelings may come up. If you practice your spirituality with a friend or group, it is highly recommended that you have someone with you during these exercises. But, if you are more comfortable, you may do this exercise on your own.

1. Prepare a massage table, cot, or bed in the middle of the floor. You may use a sleeping bag or blankets if you have no table or cot. If you are using your living room space, move the furniture so that you are lying in the middle.

2. Prepare the temple space with candles, a podium for the eulogy, and chairs for people to sit in if any are in attendance. If you do not have these things just candles are fine.

3. Lie on the table facing up. You may have a blanket or shroud covering your body and head if you like. Black or white is preferred.

4. Have your helper read the eulogy as if it is the real thing and you are actually dead or play your recording device if you are alone.

5. Take this time to play-act what it would be like if you were actually dead, and this was your funeral. What thoughts are you having? How do you feel about the whole process? Do any fears come up? What would it feel like to actually be dead?

6. Spend a few minutes in quiet meditation on this whole process after it is finished.

7. Journal your experiences.

As we are destined to be born, we are destined to die. I have heard it said that death is the great equalizer; no one can escape from it. It is because of our death that we learn to live. It is death that prompts us to live our lives fully and become spiritual human beings. Death is not meant to be easy or clean. Death is sometimes scary and dirty. However, death is a spiritual process that helps us transcend our earthly lives so that we can evolve to be more than we are now. It is designed to challenge us, but never to punish. It is through challenges that we can see just how powerful we are. When we work with death's energies, we begin to further our understanding of the roll death plays in the great cosmic design. I have found the more I work with death, the more I understand that it is essential to the Universe. Without death, the Universe could not exist. When something dies it makes way for something better to appear. This is how evolution works. Without death there could not be life. It is the ebb and flow of the Universe and of balance.

2
Ancient Ancestral Practices

Orpheus' Search for Eurydice (Greco-Roman)

There was a blessed singer named Orpheus who would play the lyre that was given to him by his father, Apollo, the god of the sun and of music. He was so skilled at song that the spirits of Heaven and Earth would often stop their daily tasks to listen to him. He married a beautiful woman named Eurydice and he loved her above all things, even his blessed songs. One day while Eurydice was walking through the fields, she was bitten on the foot by a snake and died. Orpheus' grief was so great that he could not bear to live without his Eurydice. He decided that he would go down to Hades and ask the god of the dead himself to release her. This would be no easy task.

He found a secret passage into the Underworld through the side of a mountain. He made his way down the dark tunnels and braved the ghostly residence and the monsters that lurked down below. Finally, he made his way to the throne room of Hades and Persephone. He presented the Underworld King and Queen a song. In his song, he sang about the love he had for Eurydice. He sang of his heavy grief and that he was not there to learn secrets of death or of magick, but to be reunited with his true love. The song was so beautiful and sad that the ghosts began to cry, the monsters' rage subsided, the furies wept, and even Hades began to tear. Persephone asked her husband to grant his request. Eurydice was released to Orpheus under the condition that as they left the Underworld, he would not look back upon her until they were out of Hades and into the light of day.

Orpheus made their way back up through the dark tunnels of Hades.

Through caverns and caves, they went. As they approached the entrance into the Middleworld, Orpheus forgot his promise and looked back at Eurydice to make sure she was still behind him. As he gazed upon her, she faded away to live eternally with the shades of the dead. Orpheus wanted to go back for her again, but the guardians of the Underworld would not allow him to go through a second time. For days, he stayed near the entrance of the mountain lamenting with his lyre and the spirits of the rocks and mountains would cry with him day after day.

Then one day, the Thracian Maidens were frenzied by the rights of Bacchus and went into a fury. They found Orpheus and tore him limb from limb, yet his lyre was unharmed which Zeus placed among the stars. Finally, Orpheus and Eurydice were united in death roaming together among the fields of bliss with the Ancestors.

Ancient Pagan Worship

Pagans throughout the ages have honored the Ancestors. In ancient times, the belief of an afterlife was universal. We speculate that one of the ways that the idea of an afterlife came to be was through dreams. People could go to sleep and dream of friends and loved ones who were long dead. In their dream state they would have extraordinary powers and go on exciting adventures, or even meet monsters. When they awoke, they could speak with others and confirm this unusual plane of existence. When their friends or family would die, it would appear as if they were "asleep" and that they would permanently stay in this strange and wonderful land. This land became more commonly known as the Underworld. People could observe the nature of death and decay and see how the physical body would decompose and return its essence to the Earth below. To the ancient mind, the energy and spirit of a person would follow this decomposition as their spirit would travel down below. This is one of the reasons that people believed that the Underworld was a place of horrors, skeletons, and decaying things. In some indigenous tribes, seeing that the bodies of the dead would decay and become one with the land was proof that the Ancestors joined with the land and watched over the tribe. Their energies were perceived as actually merging with the land, trees, rocks, and bodies of water. This is one of the reasons why Native American tribes honor their homeland so much and defended it with their lives. They could not stand the thought of never seeing their Ancestors again. There are as many different ways that ancient pagans honored the dead as there are different cultures. Many ancient cultures seem to have in common the belief that the dead went to a place beneath the ground.

Our Ancestors were thought to have tremendous power. The ancients believed that the Ancestors had the ability to control some of the Underworld energy and life force that comes to us in this world. They also believed that the Ancestors could intervene on their behalf with the gods. For instance, if you needed magick done for you, say to find a new love or increase prosperity, you could ask your Ancestors to speak to your deities on your behalf so that your desire would manifest. The Ancestors could also aid in healing. There are many ancient spells and charms that call upon the power of the Ancestors when using magick to heal the sick. To me, this makes perfect sense. Who is more likely to help you, some deity you rarely speak to or your great grandparents who wish only for you to be healthy and happy? Personally, this is one of the most fulfilling ways to work with the Ancestors. The Ancestors also could control good or ill fortune. Remember, the Ancestors are very close to the mystery and power of the Underworld. For those Ancestors who continued to watch over the family, they would help them in whatever way they could. It was thought that if you gave them water, food, and prayers, then the energy exchange would be given back to you with blessings and good fortune. If you had forgotten your duty to the Ancestors, then it was imperative that the Ancestors remind you of your obligations to them and give you a learning lesson. This sometimes would manifest in the form of sudden bad luck.

Ancient pagans also thought that the Ancestors could become gods themselves. In Hinduism today, it is believed that when you live your life according to dharma (the proper way to live according to honor, morals, ethics, and accepting your place in the class system) you may be freed from the cycles of reincarnation and become a god. In this philosophy, the Ancestors could not be on equal footing with great and powerful gods such as Brahma and Vishnu, but were perceived as divine, nonetheless. It was because they achieved great wisdom and transformation that they were allowed to ascend to heaven and become a god. However, each of the many heavens in Hinduism had its own lessons. If you learned the divine lessons, then you were able to ascend further up into the next heaven. If not, you could be cast down from heaven and be forced to dwell in the realm of the Ancestors in the Underworld.

It is believed that some of the Nordic Gods such as Odin, Freyr, and Thor may have been "real" Kings of northern Europe who, after their deaths, were worshiped by the people as "Kings" in the spirit world and, therefore, were transformed by local belief into Gods. In Egypt, it was believed that the god Osiris was also a King, or pharaoh, who was deified after death. In ancient Egypt, all kings were referred to as Osiris. It is thought that the basis of this myth is that one of the ancient kings of Egypt was deified. After his death, his body was dismembered, ground up, and then spread throughout the land. This act made him the god of the Underworld, Osiris. Some believe that ancient myths have historical truths in them and that the stories are a poetic account of what happened in the distant past.

Necromancy

When modern people hear the word "necromancy" they often think of grave robbing, black magick, and binding spirits to do evil things. But in fact, that is not usually the case. *Necro-* means "dead" and *-mancy* means "divination or oracle." So, *necromancy* literally means "divination of the dead." In ancient times, working with the dead for any reason was a common practice. It was not considered strange to work with Ancestors and even spirits of those whom you did not know. Most of the time, the ancients worked with the dead for the betterment of the community. It was common to believe that our Ancestors existed alongside us in our daily life. When people needed advice and wisdom about a particular situation, they would often summon a spirit of the dead and ask them their advice. It was also discovered that the Ancestors could bring many blessings and benefits to the community when given proper rites and devotions. Magicians, witches, and sorcerers learned that there were many benefits and powers to be learned from the dead. The dead can even be called upon to aid in healing rites and rituals.

Many witches also used the powers of the dead in their rituals. In ancient Greece, a type of necromancer known as a "Goes" had special powers over the dead. They were able to summon the shades and use them for prophecy and magick. It appears they were used to help the grieving contact their loved ones, but soon it was believed that they were using the dead for black magick. In fact, their necromantic magick became known as *goeteia*. This is where ceremonial magicians get the name of the Goetia, the summoning of demons. This type of magick was used during the 16th century by a witch known as Bessie Dunlop who had a spirit of the dead named Tom Reid who helped her in her witchcraft. We can speculate that many other witches used necromantic spirits to help in their magick as well.

Using the dead for prophecy was practiced in many parts of the world in many pagan cultures. For some of us it may seem odd or distasteful, but it was so much of a common practice that it was often told in myths. Most of us in the pagan community are familiar with Asatru and the Nordic pantheon. There is a myth told by the Nordics of the mighty Odin, who conjures a Volva (a seeress), who is dead to give he and the other gods prophecy of what is to come.

Ancient Egyptian Death Rites

The Ancient Egyptians left us a vast amount of information about the death and funeral rites of their people. We know a great deal about the Egyptians because they kept extensive records of their gods and the cosmos. Their priests and magicians observed the cycles of the planets and stars and the Earth upon which they lived. They believed that the physical world was a reflection of the Underworld and the Upperworld. They believed that upon death, the soul would travel into the Underworld to face many trials before a person could join their beloved gods. However, the body had to be preserved. What happened to the physical body happened to the spirit body as well. They did not want the process of decay to prevent the spirits from their tasks in the Underworld. Great preparations were made to make sure the spirits succeeded in their challenges.

Embalming

Upon death, the body was washed and then dried out with natron. It was then perfumed and dressed in linen. The embalmers were specialized priests that wore the mask of Anubis. It is speculated that these priests (whose title was Anubis, meaning priests of embalming) invoked the god into themselves so that it was not the priests who were preparing the body, but Anubis himself!

The organs were removed from the corpse. The Anubis priests began with the head and worked their way down to the feet. The brain was removed through the nose and discarded. At the time, they did not understand the significance of the brain. The other organs - the heart, liver, stomach, intestines, and pancreas – were preserved with resin, put inside magical jars, and then placed back inside the corpse.

The body was restored as much as possible to look the way it looked in life. The priests used sawdust, wax, resin, and makeup to give the body a more "alive" look. The body was perfumed again and bandaged. The bandages of the mummification process had to be wrapped in a ritual manner. The head, torso, and limbs had to be wrapped either six or seven times depending upon the magical intention. In magick, numbers have different meanings. If we use a modern interpretation of numbers; six is a number of the sun and means harmony, seven is the number of Venus and the seven ancient planets and means love or compassion. During the embalming process, prayers were given to Anubis, Osiris, Isis, and Horus to protect the Ba (astral body) of the person and aid them in their journey to Underworld, the Duat (pronounced DOO-what).

"Opening of the Mouth"

After the body was mummified, it was necessary to bring the body back to "life." Because it had a divine purpose, Egyptian necromancy, was not seen as distasteful but as a necessity for the journey ahead. This was done so that the spirit of the deceased could enjoy the offerings and festivals before its Ba journeyed into the Duat. The body was purified with incense and perfumes and given offerings of animal sacrifice. Prayers and more incense were given until the body was thought to be Osiris. To be Osiris was a title meaning "resurrected." To the Egyptians, to be resurrected meant that the astral body was given enough energy to maintain itself in the physical plane and then released into the Underworld for its journey to the realm of Ma'at.

Book of the Dead

The Book of the Dead was a term coined by archeologists when they first discovered the scrolls, or books, in the tombs of the kings. The books seem to be a part of the New Kingdom era of Egyptian history (1,500-1,070 BCE) . The correct term for the book is *The Book of Going Forth by Day*. The term *day* for the Egyptians in this context meant *going to the light* or *going into the light*—the light being the realm of the gods. The books of the dead were maps and directions on how to navigate the Underworld. There were spells, charms, and warnings about what to do to maintain power, defeat monsters, and find your way through the more frightening aspects of the Dwat. One book even told you how to handle oneself once a person finally made it to the presence of Ma'at—the goddess of Truth—and the rest of the gods. The book was an invaluable resource when journeying into the Underworld.

Greco-Roman Temples of the Dead

In Greece and Rome, if one wanted to speak to the dead in a direct way, they could go to one of the notorious Temples of the Dead. The ancient Greeks believed these temples were built over a gateway into Hades. To the ancient Greco-Romans this was just not a belief or a spiritual experience, such as one experiences when one goes to Church or Temple to "feel" the presence of God, but a literal experience of the depths of

Hades, the Underworld Gods, and the dead. These ancient people wanted a tangible experience. We must remember that to these civilizations, ghosts and the gods were not myths, but a very "real," tangible thing. These temples were built near lakes, on or near mountains, or any place that seemed to open up into the Underworld below.

Many people traveled for many miles to the temples . The temples were always isolated from the more metropolitan cities. They were kept far away from the everyday life. The dead, and all they represented, were to be left alone. Most people in Greco-Roman society looked down upon the magick of the dead. Though it was not illegal, it was frowned upon, and only the brave chose to travel to visit the oracles who dwelt in these temple complexes. The journey took several days, if not weeks, and it was usually the wealthy who were able to afford such a venture. However, the everyday person who could find payment would sometimes go to the temples as well.

If the seeker wished to consult the dead at the temple, they had to first arrange the affair with the Sybil. It was the Sybil who was the seeress and High Priestess of the Temple, who would make all the arrangements for the seeker. It was her duty to set up the ritual from beginning to end. It was she who possessed the power to open the gates of Hades and summon the shade or shades with whom the seeker wished to communicate. To have such a dark, yet profound experience came at a steep cost. The payment was seven bullocks, seven ewes, and a large amount of olive oil. Other types of payment might include cows, oxen, and rams. The temple kept its own livestock so that the journeyer could purchase them there rather than try to travel with such a burden over difficult terrain and dangerous roads. This arrangement also allowed the temple to raise money for maintenance as well as attend to the personal needs of the priests of the temple. A portion of the livestock was given as an offering to the gods. The Sybil was given wine and barley cakes as a personal offering to her.

Once the arrangements were put into place, the seeker was admitted into the underground temple. They would be given a special potion that would help him perceive the magical nature of the temple. They were led into the first room which was painted with depictions of myriad scenarios of the horrors of life. The pictures showed the effects of various diseases, old age, fear, poverty, hunger, strife, and insanity. The seeker would be left in the room alone to contemplate the images for three days to get them into the right frame of mind to continue on their journey into the Underworld temple. Imagine, for a moment, what it might have been like to stay in this room for three days for the sole purpose of contemplation. This is very much like hypnosis. Understandably, the seeker's mind would begin to accept the horrors they were seeing. The images of death, murder, battle, and disease would seep deeper and deeper into their mind. They would be given no food or water. If they slept, they were sure to have death dreams.

After the third day the seeker was brought out of the room to sacrifice a black ewe to a deity of the Underworld, who would most likely be Persephone. Most offerings and sacrifices were given to Persephone because she was the intercessor between Hades and the Midworld. She was the goddess of the dead who was able to leave the Realm of the Dead for six months out of the year. She could understand the pain and sorrow of the living and the dead, and it was she who would have sympathy with them. The priest would look at the entrails to see if it was a favorable time for the consultation of the dead. The seeker was then led to an underground river that had been built to look like the River of Forgetfulness in Hades. There, after a proper fast, the seeker would be bathed and then led to another river that was called the "water of memory." The seeker bathed in and drank these waters, which probably had hallucinogenic drugs in them. The seeker would have no idea about the herbs that were placed in the water. The hallucinogens had several purposes. One purpose was to help the seeker release any mental blocks and doubts about the process that he was about to undertake. Another purpose was to have them truly believe that what they were seeing in the temple was real. It was believed that psychotropic drugs helped a person see into the spirit world.

After this was done, they sacrificed a black ewe to the Goddess Night and to the Earth and was dressed in a white tunic with their hair bound and a belt with a bronze dagger. They were also given a sword. The sword was to protect the seeker against the shades that may be angered by their disturbance of the netherworld. They also carried a golden branch of mistletoe as an offering to Persephone.

The Sybil would be dressed in scarlet, most likely because scarlet represented the blood of the living and of life itself that some of the shades so desperately craved. This would give them energy to manifest in our world. Scarlet also symbolized her power over life and death and her rank within the Temple.

The Path

The seeker was led further into the temple. They entered an 8ft 21-inch-wide hole by a ladder that descended into a round room. They were then led through a passageway into a tunnel complex. Here priests, dressed in black wearing black headdresses, met the seeker. The priests sang and chanted eerie songs. This was done to put the seeker further into an altered state of consciousness to see the dead spirits.

The seeker continued through the tunnel until they found themself at a junction with three tunnels. As the seeker is led to the fork, the door behind them shut causing a shift in air pressure. Take a moment to imagine what the seeker must have been going through. Their mind was altered, and their surroundings were dark and frightening. The seeker carried on because they sought to confront the spirit of the dead of someone they knew, perhaps someone he loved.

The Sybil would say: "The left tunnel leads to Tartarus, the right to the House of Persephone." A priest hidden in the left tunnel would scream and burn harsh-smelling incense as a sign of torment. The seeker was led to the right tunnel down into yet another tunnel and then to the River Styx. The tunnel was filled with 100 lamps for illumination. We do not know exactly what the lamps were for, but my theory is that one, it was to give the tunnels an "Otherworldly" illumination and two, may have represented the spirits who dwelled in Hades. To the seeker, this must have been a fantastic and eerie sight!

At the River Styx, the seeker was led to another priest that was personifying Charon, the ferryman. His appearance was like an ancient filthy demon. Once on the other side of the river, a dog barked ferociously to represent Cerberus. This was a trained dog that recognized the Sybil.

They then went up steep stairs to another level and down a corridor. Then the seeker left the mistletoe in a niche in the wall as an offering to Persephone. In the inner sanctum, there was an altar with a tied up sacrificial animal. A priest cut its throat and let the blood poor to the ground for the shades. It is important to remember that the ancient view of sacrifice was different than our own. It was not looked down upon in ancient times to kill animals for their blood to give to the spirits of the dead. It was believed that the energy or life force of blood would give spirits of the dead, or shades, energy to manifest physically in the Middleworld.

After the blood was spilled, the shades would appear. Another priest would act as a medium. It is believed that the priests may have used elaborate costumes to invoke or aspect the spirits of the dead. The spirit of the dead that the seeker wished to speak to would then "manifest." They would then answer the seeker's questions. Sometimes the seeker would receive answers in a clear direct manner, sometimes not. After a while, to end the session the vast shades of the dead would appear to come out and overcrowd the spirit. This was done by other priests who would dress in all black, making horrible noises to frighten the seeker which would make them want to end the session quickly. To the seeker this was perceived as the many shades of the dead that were gathering around to taste the lifeforce (blood) that was nearby. When this happened, the seeker was then escorted out through a secret tunnel. The priest would warn them not to look back or else they would have to stay eternally in Hades. The seeker would then arrive at the room near the entrance. The Sybil and the priest went over what was said in the session so that the seeker understood what was trying to be communicated to them.

The Kidnapping of Persephone

One day, Demeter, Goddess of the fields and agriculture, and her daughter, Persephone, were picking lilies and violets. While they were enjoying the beautiful day, Hades, the God of the Underworld, gazed upon her. He became enamored by her beauty and could think of nothing but having her as his Queen. He quickly grabbed her and carried her away on his chariot. Persephone screamed in terror and her mother came running after her. Before Demeter could see her daughter being carried away, Hades used his magical trident to create a hole in the side of the mountain, a gateway down into the Underworld. Persephone was lost.

Demeter mourned the loss of Persephone. For days she walked the Earth in great sadness not knowing what had happened to her daughter.

In her mourning, the land began to dry up, the fields withered, and the cold dark skies covered the land. Snows fell for the first time. Then, a water nymph came to Demeter and told her that she had seen Hades kidnap Persephone and take her down into the Underworld. Upon hearing this news, Demeter flew right away to Olympus to give her grievance to Zeus. Zeus understood her grief and the unfairness of the kidnapping. He promised to bring Persephone from the Underworld if she did not have anything to eat or drink there. Hermes, the messenger of the gods, was sent down into the Underworld and told Hades of Zeus' demand to release Persephone. Hades complied. But before Persephone left the gates of Hades, he gave her a pomegranate to subdue her hunger for the long trip back to the Middleworld. She then ate the pomegranate seeds, not knowing her fate. The Fates themselves could not undo what was set into motion by Hades. Zeus had to explain to Demeter what had happened. However, Zeus took pity on Demeter and Persephone and agreed to a compromise. For half the year Persephone had to remain in the Underworld as the Queen of Hades, but for the rest of the year could go back to her mother in the Middleworld. Demeter agreed to this compromise. But, whenever Persephone returned to the Underworld, Demeter would once again walk the Earth with sadness and winter would return to the world.

Rites of Eleusis

The Eleusinian Mysteries are perhaps the most famous rituals in the ancient world. People would travel vast distances to be able to partake in the most sacred mysteries of the ancient, civilized world. These rites were akin to a scholar going to graduate school to receive a degree that would put you in the ranks of other great scholars. Many philosophers and even the god of healing, Aesculapius, was said to have gone through the mysteries. It was thought that to obtain an adequate idea of the gods and spirituality, one must go through the Eleusinian Mysteries. It was expected that both men and women were to be initiated. These rites were so sacred and so secret, that it was forbidden to speak of these rites with anyone who was uninitiated to the Eleusinian Mysteries. The punishment for doing so was death. And, indeed, punishment was carried out.

The Greeks most certainly kept written records of their philosophies, histories, and magick, however, there are no written records of the Rites of Eleusis. Remember, if the uninitiated found out about the rituals, they would face the punishment of death. The only records we have about the ritual are from art, such as pictures on vases, the occasional testimonial from a seeker of the mysteries, and those who spoke too much in front of non-initiates after too much drink. Archeologists and historians have spent many years trying to piece it all together.

It is believed that the mysteries were broken up into two sections, the Lesser and Greater Mysteries. The Lesser Mysteries began with the sacrifice of cattle to Persephone and Demeter. Before one could begin initiation, they had to fast for a certain number of days and keep their spirits and bodies as pure as possible. Essentially, there were three degrees. The first degree instructed the seeker in the myths of Demeter and Persephone and the rituals in which they should be honored.

For the second degree of initiation, the seeker was led into the temple. Their hands were purified with consecrated water. The priest led them into the first chamber. The candidates were locked into a dark room. The temple transformed into Hades itself. The sounds of the dead could be heard. Sorrowful sounds of morning, pain, and dread was heard from all sides. The shades of the dead were coming to get them! The door of Tartarus was opened, and all the demons and monsters of Hades could be seen. There were reports that the actual demons and monsters of legend materialized before them! In each of the cold, dark rooms the candidates were pushed, pulled, and hit by the beings of the Hades looking for life. Somehow the seekers had to make it through. They could hear the painful laments of the shades who died from war, disease, murder, and accident. The dead were coming closer and closer to the seekers. They had to keep moving all the while suffering the brutal pushing and beatings of the demons of Hades. Finally, as they cleared the last chamber, the door of Tartarus was closed. The dark spirits and monsters were shut back into the dark corners of Hades. At last, a light was illuminated. The lights shone on a great statue of Demeter, the goddess of agriculture. Nature spirits danced around her with much joy! The initiate now understood the joys of living. Hades is a place of the sorrowful dead. Pain and suffering are all you would find there. It was discovered by the initiates that through living a life well lived, that Demeter granted blessing in this life, not the next. Life was meant to be joyful even in the midst of pain and suffering here on Earth. Demeter would sustain us all!

During the festival, the sacred marriage took place. A high priestess and high priest would invoke either Demeter and Zeus or Persephone and Hades to perform the sacred act of ritual sex to ensure the union of the divine to one another.

The third degree held the mystery of the ear of grain (wheat). The candidate, who was ready for the final degree, was taught about the magical properties of the ear of grain and its significant with the regeneration powers of Demeter. This final degree taught that during the quest for enlightenment, demons and monsters of the candidate's own making would try to sabotage them from obtaining the truth of the gods and the universe. What this means is that the candidate's personal fears, weaknesses, and imbalances would be revealed. The candidate must understand that these are the things that keep them from discovering personal growth and enlightenment. They would learn that the universe had a creator and that the gods were mortal men and women who had ascended to godhood. The initiates were taught that through death and enlightenment one could ascend to become immortal and divine. That those trapped in Hades, under the protection of Persephone, would never ascend and become greater than their fates had prescribed for them.

Exercise:
Meditation of the Ear of Grain and Regeneration

Sit in a comfortable position. Take a deep breath and allow the stresses of the day to fade away as you exhale. Take another deep breath and as you exhale, allow the muscles in your body to relax. Take one more deep breath and allow the chatter in your mind to fade away. Close your eyes. Be at one with peace.

Visualize yourself in a barren field. The ground beneath you is hard and cold and you can smell the clay of the Earth. There is nothing around you for miles and miles. It is night, and the stars above are bright and magnificent. You walk through this barren land. This is the place where the ancients would plant their wheat, but that was thousands of years ago. As far as you can tell, there is no life now. No life. Only the harsh Earth below and the black sky of night filled with the stars. You feel a faint call to your heart. Something is leading you to the very center of the barren field. The soil cracks and crumbles as you trample upon it. It has not rained for so awfully long.

As you finally make it to the center of the dark field, you realize that you have discovered a great treasure. There is one single stalk of wheat growing in the lifeless place. Somehow it has survived. In all the death that is around you, you have found one single piece of life. You sit down on the ground touching the lonely stalk of wheat. As you sit and place your hands on the wheat you feel the faint call of Demeter, the goddess of agriculture. It is more of a call to your heart than to your ears. You look up to the celestial heavens and the stars seem so much brighter now. They seem to be waiting for you to do something. But what?

As you sit upon the cold ground your eyes become better focused in the blackness of night. You then can faintly make out a few grave markers, old rusty guns, and fragments of some kind of machine; is that an army helmet you see? You realize that you sit upon a battlefield from ages ago. Was there a war that had taken place on the field that once supported life with wheat to feed the people? Death was once here and even death has gone away.

You connect your energies to the stalk of wheat. You feel its life-force pulsing through the roots and up the stalk to the leaves and grains. Take a moment to meditate with the wheat and your surroundings. What does the wheat tell you? What does the Earth itself have to say? What do the stars tell you? Take as much time as you need.

When you are finished, journal your experience.

The Ghost Dance

The Ghost Dance is a spiritual technique practiced by some Lakota and other Native American tribes from the plains region of the United States. The Ghost Dance is more than a Native style of dancing. It is considered a religion unto itself. The Ghost Dance was given to a Lakota Healer named Jack Wilson in a vision. During the dance, the dancers evoke the spirits of the Ancestors to come and dance with them. By doing so, the spirits of the dead are "resurrected" in spirit form. This is done to bring the spirits back from the land of the dead so that they may aid the people with their troubles in life such as food, shelter, tribal matters, and disputes over land with the United States government. It was believed that the wisdom and power of the Ancestors would help guide the tribes to a better future.

There were many tensions between the Native American people of the plains and the United States government. All of the treaties were broken one by one, and the land allotted to the Lakota people by the U.S. became smaller and smaller. In one instance, men found gold in the Black Hills region, which at the time belonged to the Lakota. The government soon took that land away from the Lakota because of the profits that could be given to the U.S. The U.S. military wanted the Lakota people to stay on the reservations. The Lakota, being a nomadic tribe, followed the bison wherever the herds went. In response to this, the U.S. military attempted to wipe out the bison. Luckily, a few bison remained, and their population eventually increased. In the late 1800s, however, the bison were nearly all destroyed, and the Lakota were starving. They were forced to do what the U.S. wanted them to do. They were angry at the way the treaties were broken and their people were left to become sick and die of starvation and cold. The native peoples felt hopeless.

During the winter of 1889 there was a solar eclipse that caused great unease among the Native American Plains people. The natives living at that time did not know what a solar eclipse was and were very afraid of the giant spirit that blocked out the light of the sun. Some were so afraid that they shot their rifles at the shadow trying to kill it or at least move it away from the sun. As the sun became dark, a Lakota healer named Jack Wilson became deathly ill. As he lay in his bed, his spirit flew up to the Heavens and there the Creator gave him a vision. In his vision, the people danced the Ghost Dance. By living a virtuous Native life, making peace with the Whites, and not going to war, the Ancestors would return and assist the people in gaining back their spirituality, their tribal power, and their lands. When Jack Wilson awoke, he taught the people this powerful dance. He taught the people that by walking the "good red road" and living a "good honest life" the Ancestors would return from the land of the dead and give the people power over themselves and their lives.

In Native American customs, the Ancestors were always remembered and honored. For the Natives, the land of the dead was simply hidden from view by a veil, and yet was all around us. The Ancestors were always with us, but the Ghost Dance gave the people the energy and power to summon the Ancestors in a more tangible way to help guide the tribe. The Ghost Dance became a religion. Jack Wilson would "preach" his teachings to anyone who would listen. Many Native people came to hear him speak and were profoundly moved by his vision and the idea of the return of the Ancestors. The people would then report back to their tribes of the wonder and power of the Ghost Dance. The Ghost Dance caught on throughout the U.S. Plains region.

The U.S. government heard rumors of this Ghost Dance and thought it nothing more than superstitions of the primitive peoples. However, they did notice that the once broken Native people were becoming empowered again. It may be helpful to remember that the white soldiers were Christian and thought of the Native spirituality as nonsense at best and devil worship at worst. They took great pains to break the spirits of the Natives and were profoundly upset when the Natives began to regain their personal power and will. The control of the Native People became more and more difficult. They even went so far as to tell their soldiers that the Ghost Dance was supposed to call up the dead so that they could push back the White people to take back their lands. If any Native People believed this, which is unlikely, it was not based upon the teachings of Jack Wilson.

The Ghost Dance religion became more and more popular and

practiced throughout the Western United States. The Lakota people on the Pine Ridge reservation freely danced the Ghost Dance and became more and more defiant of the ruling military stationed there. Tensions were high between the Lakota people and the military at Pine Ridge. Each side mistrusted the other and the soldiers were looking for any reason they could to kill and destroy the natives. Sitting Bull was a defiant Lakota Chief who was looking out for the best interest of his people. The soldiers came to arrest him, and one anxious Lakota man shot his riffle. The soldier shot Sitting Bull at point blank range in the head. Sitting Bull's horse was trained to trot when he heard gunshots. When the horse seemed to dance the Natives took that as a sign as the return of the Ancestors of the Ghost Dance. Shots were fired on both sides. 153 Lakota were killed that day. This would be known as the Massacre at Wounded Knee.

Whites feared the Ghost Dance not because they feared the return of the spirits, but because it represented the empowerment of a people whom they were trying to destroy. The massacre was brought on by hate, racism, and fear. The Ghost Dance religion taught tribal values and abstinence from war. Many Natives died during this time of being forced onto reservations and having little to no food and shelter. The Lakota, as well as many other tribes who took to the Ghost Dance, were rejoicing in the fact that they could dance with their lost loved ones, and they could once again become part of the tribal community. There are other shamanic cultures that teach a form of dancing with the Ancestors. What made the Ghost Dance stand out is the way that Jack Wilson preached about the values of a "good clean life" and how it would empower the people once more.

Exercise: Dancing With the Ancestors

Dancing with the Ancestors is a very empowering practice. Whenever I dance on a dance floor or around a drum circle, I always make sure I dance a little bit with the Ancestors who are willing to dance with me. I will say, almost always the Ancestors want to dance with you. The more you work with your Ancestors, the more you will notice when they appear more prominently in your energy field. The Ancestors, being energy themselves, can easily incorporate themselves in your aura. When our gods and Ancestors have a strong connection with us, they connect with our energies and give us strength, power, and guidance upon our spiritual paths. The Ancestors are always there, but we have to take the time to notice them. Dancing with the Ancestors is one of the best and most fun ways of working with them. When you first start dancing with your Ancestors, begin with music that has a simple beat. Any type of music that makes you feel spiritual will do as long as it has nice beat to it. There are a few things to keep in mind when dancing with your ancestors. Your ancestors will still have the same likes and dislikes when it comes to music. Remember, your grandmother who did not like heavy metal in life will not like it in death. However, I have noticed that even if tribal music was not something they listened to in life they will enjoy it in death. Most likely, this is because the drumbeat, which represents the heartbeat of the Earth, is a universal phenomenon and resonates through all of time and space. This is one of the reasons why we can travel astrally so freely with a shamanic drumbeat. The Ancestors appreciate new music too, but you may need to experiment with this a little bit before you find the right kind of music for them. Also, be aware that some ancestors may like one type of music while others will hate it, and vice versa. Try to find something that most of them can agree on unless you are working with one specific ancestor.

1. Light the candle on your Ancestor altar and say a prayer for your Ancestors in the usual manner. Fill the water bowls with water. Instructions on how to create an ancestor altar are in chapter 3.

2. Explain to your Ancestors that you would like to share energy with them by dancing with them.

3. Turn on the music of your choice. I light additional candles for ambiance, but this is a personal preference and you may do as feels appropriate to you. If you like, you can light incense such as sage or any other scent that makes you feel magical and connected with your Ancestors.

4. Begin slowly swaying back and forth with the music. Circle around the room with the rhythm of the music. Allow yourself to go into a light trance. Try not to go into a heavy trance until you are used to dancing with the Ancestors. We do not want you to fall down!

5. Visualize your Ancestors dancing with you. See them swaying back and forth with the music as you do. You may hold their hands if you wish, but this is not necessary. Do what feels right to you. The energy exchange will be stronger if you hold hands, but they will still receive energy from you and you from them if you do not hold hands.

6. Continue to dance as long as you wish. During the dance try to connect to the energies of your Ancestors as best you can. All the energies will flow around you and into your heart. At the end of your dance, thank your Ancestor for dancing with you and sharing this experience.

7. When you are ready, say your goodbyes to them and blow out the candles.

Exercise: Ancestor Dance Ritual

In my religious group, The Fellowship of the Phoenix, we have a yearly ritual around Samhain called Shadowdance. In this ritual, our focus is calling upon the Ancestors and connecting to them on a deeper level. The veil is thin at this time of year, so it is much easier for novices to do ancestor work if they have never had training. Our rituals are public, so we invite the greater public to participate. Each year we try to perform a different ceremony, but the core is the same, dancing with the Ancestors. We call to our ancestors in every ritual, but during Shadowdance our main focus is dancing with our beloved dead and the hidden company of the witches. This ritual is great fun and I encourage you to create a ceremony with simply yourself, a group of friends, or your religious group to share in power of magick with the Ancestors.

When organizing the Ancestor Dance Ritual, it is important that everyone involved understand what is to occur. You are going to summon the Ancestors through communal dance and connect with them on an energetic personal level. It is better to perform this dance with friends and colleagues who share your same spiritual philosophies. This is one of the easiest ways to work with the Ancestors. Many cultures have been doing this sort of dancing for all of human history. These cultures, however, have been taught from birth that working with the Ancestors is a fulfilling spiritual practice and there is nothing to be frightened of. In our modern society, as we have learned, people do not honor the dead and do not believe that their spirits stay close to us. When performing this dance with others it must be with the understanding that the Ancestors who show up are there because they love us. It does occur that sometimes novices or people inexperienced with Ancestor work have a strong tangible connection to the dead who come to dance with us. For some, this may be frightening or unnerving. It is best to have experienced magicians and clergy on hand to help people who may have trouble or fears with this practice.

When it comes to public dances at a drum circle or Neo-pagan gathering, especially with the Ancestor Dance, remind people that drugs are never a good idea. Drugs alter the mind in a way that distorts the energies, and the mind can have a difficult time interpreting what is happening around them.

1. You may perform this ritual indoors or outdoors with a small bonfire or lantern. You can have one person or as many as you like. As a ritual facilitator, it might be wise to begin with a smaller group. You will have to keep an eye on the energies that are being summoned and hold space for the group.

2. I think it is important to give offerings to the Ancestors such as food, flowers, and other gifts. You can place them on a sacred space or altar, or place them directly on the ground outside of the dance space

3. You may use tribal or spiritual music or anything with a nice beat that makes you want to trance out and summon the ancestors. The music can be recorded our performed live with drummers or other musicians.

4. Begin by having the participants start swaying to the beat. They may begin moving into a circle in a clockwise (sunwise) manner.

5. Ask them to think about a specific Ancestor, or simply one of their Ancestors who wishes to join in the dance.

6. As they circle around, have them take a breath in and exhale energy next to them to allow the Ancestor to manifest for them. To do this successfully, they must have a deep longing desire to have the

spirit of their loved one to dance with them. It may help to open the heart chakra and send the Ancestors heart centered energy. Have everyone visualize the Ancestors dancing with them. The more desire one has, the more tangible the experience will be for each person.

7. If someone does not feel an Ancestor next to them, that is okay. Learning to feel the spirits around us often takes time and practice. Simply knowing the Ancestors are dancing with them will work just as well. Remind each dancer to visualize the Ancestors to the best of their ability.

8. Some of the dancers may receive visions or insights. Some may have wonderful conversations with their Ancestors, while others will simply have a wonderful energy exchange experience.

9. This is very healing and many sorts of emotions can come up. Joy, happiness, ecstasy, and perhaps even grief. Try to keep this as joyful as possible. If you notice someone grieving and unable to dance, gently guide them to the edge of the circle and either you or another helper can speak to them, or better yet listen to what they have to say. If they do not wish to speak, simply being there with them for support is perhaps all they need.

When you observe that the dancing is winding down or perhaps people are becoming very tired, you may end the dance. Give thanks to the Ancestors and each other for a wonderful experience.

For those of us practice an ancient religion or practice magick, Ancestor honoring is part of our heritage. As we have learned, ancient cultures from around the world honored the ancestors in some way. Death was an important part of the lives of ancient people. They did not run from it, they embraced it with both arms, heart, and soul. The dead and their magick was important for the survival of the community. Without the dead, the village or tribe would surely fail. It was also the mysteries of death and the ancestors that taught us the value of life.

3
Honoring Our Ancestors

Those Who Come From The Mountain (Japan/Shinto)

The snow hasn't fallen yet tonight. I suppose it will. It usually does all through the month of January. So cold. Mother convinced me to come out here to the rice fields, reluctantly, I might add. Grandmother is getting old; she says this may be her last time to see the Ancestors come down from the mountain. I have never seen such a thing, but my grandmother still believes. In such modern times, why she would want to hold on to old superstition is beyond me. But we love her, and she is very stubborn when we ask her not to do something she wants to do. I think she wants to catch a glimpse of Grandfather. I personally think doing this is silly. Mother never asked me to do this thing before. Neither did Grandmother. They mostly let me do what I want, but this year they are being very weird about it. Fine. I hope whatever we are doing doesn't take long.

The rice fields look cold, bare, and empty. Not much here to see but hard ground and the promise of snow. Everyone Grandmother knows is here, all the elders in the community. They seem happy, I guess. I don't know. This all seems strange to me. The sun has finally set behind the mountain so maybe we can get this going. The sooner it starts, the sooner I can go home. The wind seems to pick up from over the Mountains. I can hear it from where I am standing. That's weird. Usually, I can't hear the wind from that far away. Grandmother used to tell us stories about how the Ancestors lived inside the mountain. She would pray to the spirits of our family who she believed lived in the mountain. She said that if we prayed to the Great Spirit of the Dead, he would help our Ancestors become great spirit guides and spirit helpers in the village. The wind seems to be getting louder now. It is pushing in the nighttime fog over the village.

The fog rolls down the mountain and sweeps through the countryside and begins getting closer to the rice fields. The old women are happy about this. "What's going on?" I ask Grandmother.

"They are coming," she says to me in a hushed voice. "They will be here soon."

"The Ancestors?" I ask.

"Shhh!" She startles me with her impatience.

The fog comes closer and closer to the fields. It seems to have a brightness about it, like it is glowing in the dark. That's weird. Perhaps a streetlight from the village is making it look like that. But the village seems too far away for that to happen. Weird. The fog is suddenly stopping over the rice fields. Did the wind stop? No, it can't really be the Ancestors. Can it?

"Look closely," Grandmother points to the fog. "There they are…"

I can kind of make out what looks like a silhouette of … people. The fog seems to be taking the form of people. Are these our Ancestors? Maybe this is a trick. Maybe Grandmother's stories have finally gotten to me. I cannot make out their faces, but I can see people made of fog walking over to the rice fields.

"They will mix their Kami, their spirits, with the rice fields for a better harvest," Grandmother says. "They will infuse their energy with the rice to ensure that our harvest is plentiful this year. Then they will return to the mountain after the crops are harvested."

I don't know what to say. Maybe Grandmother is right. Maybe our Ancestors are never gone but stay with us watching over the village as spirit guides just like the old folk say in their stories. Maybe. Maybe I'm just seeing things. But …maybe she is right.

Modern Pagan Honoring of the Dead

Honoring the beloved dead is one of the most important parts of neo-pagan and magical spirituality. We often honor our gods and goddesses and even nature spirits, but sometimes forget the most important spirits to honor, our beloved dead. Our Ancestors are our family. They are our grandmothers and grandfathers and our great-grandmothers and great-grandfathers before that. They hold an energetic and magical link to us. We may not realize it, but there is a current of power that goes from us to our ancestors and from them back to us. It is strong. It is powerful. It is the bond of family. For Pagans, it is important to not only remember our Ancestors, but to incorporate them into our daily lives. Honoring the Ancestors is a part of our sacred duty as spiritual people. Archeologists believe that one of the very first spiritual things attributed to ancient peoples is honoring the dead. Working with the dead is a part of our spiritual makeup. It is who we are as human beings.

For modern people, to ignore the Ancestors is to ignore their own heritage both physically and energetically. If we do not nurture our bond to our Ancestors, then the spiritual energy in our bodies becomes weak and spiritual blocks may develop. A lot of people go their entire lives without developing a connection. In my experience, when the ancestral bond is weak in a family, then family problems become more common in that family. For instance, family karma cannot be resolved very quickly. The family is forced to deal with the energetic "backlash" of energy until someone in the family takes action. This could be one of the reasons that members of the same family often seem to have the same habits or bad luck. They have cut themselves off from a free flow of energy and the current is blocked. It is far better to maintain a good solid connection with our Ancestors, both for our family and ourselves.

In the past, working with our Ancestors was very much a community-based effort. They were believed to continue to be a part of the community even after death. Our modern view of death and the afterlife has changed quite a bit. It is modern pagans and indigenous cultures that are continuing this age-old tradition of Ancestor-honoring. Now in modern times, working with the Ancestors has become more of an individual practice versus a communal one. However, there are still pagan groups and indigenous tribes that are re-establishing that magical current between the living and the dead. Our modern purposes for working and honoring our Ancestors may vary from our forefathers. We no longer have elaborate temples or groves dedicated to our Ancestors. In ancient times we had temples that lead into caves and the earth. These temples were used to contact the dead and the Underworld Gods. The Temple of the Dead in Baia is one such temple. The best we have in our modern society are cemeteries and mausoleums. These are wonderful places to work with the dead, but it is more powerful for our purposes if we build a family ancestral shrine.

The ancestral shrine is an altar or sacred space that is set up in your home. This acts as a focal point for you and your Ancestors to commune with each other. I like to think of it as a sort of "light house" that beckons the Ancestors to you. The Ancestors may not find it easy to navigate their way to us from the Underworld. The spiritual energy that you put into the ancestral altar calls to them. This is why when we build our shrines, we put photos and objects that belonged to our Ancestors. Not only does it help us tune into them, but it also helps them tune into us. It is very much a spiritual battery that has many benefits!

When building an ancestral shrine, it is important to remember that it is for your benefit as well as the benefit of your Ancestors. It must be in a prominent place in your home such as the living room, dining room, or kitchen. We should treat the Ancestors as we would an honored guest in our home. Just because they have no physical body does not mean we do not treat them the same. Think of it like this, if you were to have your grandmother over to your home, you would not stick her in a closet and then go about your daily routine. This is how you must view your Ancestors when you begin to work with them. They become a permanent resident in your home. I have seen in some spiritual/magical traditions where the Ancestors are only honored around Halloween or the pagan holy day of Samhain. Though this is a holy day for the Ancestors, it is far more powerful to honor the Ancestors every day! Your Ancestors are with you always; it is up to you how strongly you would like their presence felt. Remember, the more we honor the Ancestors, the more they will have an influence in this world and the Underworld. To honor them only once or twice a year is like calling your grandparents once or twice a year then asking them to buy you a new car. The chances of that happening are slim.

We should take a moment from thinking about the Ancestors energetically and think of them emotionally. Just because they are dead does not mean they have necessarily evolved to such a state that they have understanding and patience with human mistakes, frailties, and simple lack of courtesies. If we ignore our Ancestors, especially those of us who know they are here still with us, then it will hurt their feelings and potentially cause them to become angry with us. This could cause more blocks and family karma for you and your family. If for nothing else, it is good karma and energy to give honor to those who gave you their very blood.

The ancestral shrine itself should be something pleasing to you. It can be on the fireplace mantle or on a bookshelf. It can be on a little table somewhere in your living room. I have seen examples where people have placed their shrine on top of a family heirloom such as a china cabinet or end table that was in the family for generations. Some of us are not that fortunate, so any table that feels energetically acceptable will do. The shrine should feel like it is a natural part of the living area. It can be as intricate or simple as you like. I find that in the beginning, when you first build the shrine, you make it the way you want. Then the Ancestor will tell you what they like and do not like. This is perfectly fine!

I will caution on one thing when making an ancestral shrine. It should be comfortable for both you and your Ancestors. It should not be designed in such a way that looks scary or like something out of a horror movie. I am not trying to squash individual taste or other spiritual traditions but hanging plastic bats and putting frightening things on your shrine may make your Ancestors a little uneasy. With that, in Vodou and some witchcraft groups, they may use skulls and bones and items of that nature. This is fine if your spiritual tradition holds these things as sacred. The more sacred you feel your shrine is the more sacred it will become. Even so, ask the Ancestors if they are pleased with the shrine.

Building an Altar

The Ancestors have the ability to watch over us and offer us guidance and wisdom. As we have learned, just because we cannot see the influence that they have on us directly does not mean that they are not helping us in a significant spiritual way. As we work with the energy of our Ancestors, we will be able to see the influence that they have more profoundly. To do this, we must create a sacred space for them in our homes. This is commonly referred to as an Ancestral altar. At first, this idea of building an altar to the dead may seem strange. There are many religions in which ancestral altars and devotions are performed. I think it may help to clear up some misconceptions about the Ancestral altar and the work ahead. First, we are not "worshiping" our dead as one would a god. However, this was certainly done in some pagan societies because it was sometimes believed that when a person died, they became divine and protected the tribe or clan in a very powerful way. The altar is a sacred space in your home that acts as a focal point for you and your Ancestors to commune with each other. Over time, this is the place where a lot of your power for magick will come from. To have an Ancestral altar in your home will only help you build your connection with your Ancestors and develop your magical practice.

As we build our Ancestor altar, we need to keep in mind the reality of the Ancestors themselves. The spirits of the dead in our contemporary society are most likely not magical or a part of the "spiritual community". Therefore, it is probable that they are not used to working with the living in such a direct way. Sometimes, the Underworld can be disorienting and a very tricky business for the recently deceased. The concept of space and time, according to the dead's point of view, has changed dramatically from what they knew when they were living. Also, no one is magically transformed into this "all-knowing" or "all powerful" being upon death. I was once told as a child that when you died you knew everything that ever was and everything that ever will be. In my experience with working with the spirits of the dead, and the experience of my colleagues, this is simply not the case. When a person dies, their hopes, fears, desires, and prejudices remain intact. And NO, they do not know everything. However, as we discussed before, they do have a front seat view to the upcoming events that are soon to happen in our physical world. But this too, is something that the dead must learn to do. In the Underworld, spirits are taught by divine Ancestors and spirit helpers who help them acclimate to the Underworld. Part of this acclimation is learning to understand that in the world of spirit, time and space are not the same as the physical world. The dead can see the past and the future, as well as things in the present that we cannot. But, again, all these things take time and training.

Imagine for a moment that you have died, and you are trying to figure out the whole new Universe of the Underworld. Without proper training (such as a book of the dead), you may be confused and not understanding fully what is happening to you. Most of today's society come from a patriarchal religious view with either Heaven or Hell. We either are with God or the Devil. The fact is, that when we die, we do not necessarily go to the world of the divine. We go to the land of the Ancestors. A place of rejuvenation and healing. When most people die, this is confusing to them because they expect Heaven or Hell. The newly dead will need help navigating this new world of the afterlife. Also, the newly dead do not know everything. They are the same person they were when alive, the only difference being that now they are dead. When we are first beginning to work with the dead, have compassion for them and understand that sometimes they are just as confused as we are, if not more so. Often, they are surprised you are able to summon them back to the physical world. We need to help them out physically, magically, energetically, and emotionally. The best way to begin this process is to create an altar. This will help them focus on where you are. As you do your devotions and prayers to your Ancestors, the connection between you will become stronger and stronger. Over time, you will feel the power of the Ancestors and they will feel yours. Eventually, you will be able to have them perform divination for you, they will be able to help protect you and your home, and they will have other abilities you have yet to discover.

We will begin to build our family ancestral altar. As we journey through this process, it is important to know that it is a holy and magical experience. We are not looking for ingredients for a spell or ritual. We are designing a vessel so that our family's spiritual lineage can come through in a profound and powerful way. Many spiritual and religious traditions may have specific ways to set up an ancestral altar. I will explain how to build your altar in the way I was taught. The instructions I give you are merely guidelines. Please feel free to design an altar according to your spiritual beliefs and preferences. You may also notice over time that your Ancestor altar evolves and grows as you evolve and grow spiritually. Or perhaps it will be designed according to the will and wishes of the dear Ancestors who love you. This is fine. Here are the steps to get you started:

1. First, go through your family's genealogy or family tree and decide which of the Ancestors are appropriate for your altar. Start with three or, perhaps, at most four. They can be from your mother's side, father's side, or both. If you are adopted, you can certainly use your ancestors from your adapted family. You may find that one Ancestor may come through very strongly while others may not. This is normal. Do not worry about who may be the strongest or more powerful spiritually. You want to choose the Ancestor that feels compatible with your energies. Do what feels right to you. Do a divination to see if that Ancestor is right for your altar. You may use runes, the tarot, or a pendulum to determine which Ancestors are best suited to be there. Any Ancestor who does not like you, or who do not approve of your lifestyle, sexual orientation, or religious choices may not be the best fit for your altar. However, the Ancestors love to be a part of your life and I've seen spirits of the dead put aside their prejudices so that they may commune with you.

2. Once you have decided which Ancestors to put on your altar, try to

obtain photos of your Ancestors and any personal items such as watches, jewelry, or something that may fit on an altar that would be appropriate to place in public view. It is better to make sure there is one person per photograph. The reason for this is that when you work with the spirits and gaze upon their picture you are giving them energy from your heart and mind. By having more than one person in a photo you may inadvertently give energy to Ancestors who you may not necessarily want on your altar. When you do this, they will be drawn to your altar, and this may or may not be appropriate for your other Ancestors.

3. In front of each picture, place one small offering bowl for water and another offering bowl for food. Each Ancestor should have his or her own offering bowls. Try not to mix them up between Ancestors. Over time, the Ancestors will have their own energy signatures on their items, and they will not want to have the wrong food and water dish. The bowls vibrate with the energy of that Ancestor, and they do not like it when they do not have their own bowl. The Ancestors are not used to this type of spiritual work and need to adjust to the energies that they are receiving for nourishment. It may take them a while to connect with the energies of the physical world again. It is better to make sure they have their own items so that they receive the energy you are offering in a more tangible way. If you like, you can take a marker or ink pen and write their name or initials at the bottom of their dishes to help you distinguish whose dish is whose.

4. At this point you will want to obtain one central candle for the altar. The candle serves a few purposes. First, it impresses on your consciousness that the presence of your Ancestors are here when you light the candle. It also gives them spiritual energy so that they

can manifest in your physical space more easily. I find a large, white candle works well. I also love beeswax, but larger beeswax candles can become expensive. I would refrain from getting scented candles unless your Ancestors specifically ask for them. Scented candles usually contain chemical perfumes that can hinder the energies of the spirits. I, personally, get unscented candles and place a few drops of peppermint essential oil in the wax and then anoint the candle itself. Peppermint is one of the essential oils that the Ancestors love, and it will give them power.

You may make the altar as elaborate or as simple as you like. The altar should be placed in the living room or a room where people gather to visit and be with each other. We want the Ancestors to be with us in spirit just as you would if they were in a physical body. You would never invite your great grandmother to your home, sit her in a hallway or bedroom, and then visit with everyone else in the living room or den. This is considered just as rude in the spiritual world as it is in the physical world. If you have roommates, explain to them that this is a religious practice. Most roommates do not have a problem with this. If you discover there is a problem, you may need to re-evaluate your living environment. I, personally, prefer to keep my ancestral altar simple, but if you would like to add decorations that make it feel "homey" and welcoming, feel free. Just be sure that it is not too cluttered so that when working with the altar and the Ancestors, you, and they, are not distracted by too many things getting in the way. Once you build your altar and have decided who to place upon it, let it sit for a couple of days so that it may find its grounding in the physical and spiritual worlds.

Honoring and Devotion

Before giving offerings to our beloved dead, set up your altar, light your ancestral candle and say a prayer to the gods and higher spirits on their behalf. You can say something to the effect of, "I ask the Gods to grant blessings, peace, and spiritual evolution to my Ancestors (name), (name), and (name)." Make sure you use their full names. This strengthens their connection to you, the altar, and your energies and spirits. Say this prayer every day for at least a week before engaging in conversation with your Ancestors. This will give your Ancestors time to acclimatize to the new altar and helps them understand that this is a focal point for energy and connection with you. Your Ancestors will hear your prayers in the Underworld. It is my belief that once you have decided to create the ancestral altar and work with them, the magical/spiritual connection begins to be made, however faintly. During your first initial prayers to and for the Ancestors, the energies and higher beings are preparing your Ancestors to come to the physical plane and work with you.

After a week or so, you may begin giving your Ancestors the offering of water in their water bowl. Different traditions will have different ways of doing this. In some, it is believed that it is better to give the Ancestors water after you speak with them. In others, you only put the water in after they speak with you. This is done to encourage them to speak and to overcome the astral/energy challenges which may block them from speaking with you. I understand this in principle, but to me the Ancestors should be honored whether they speak to you or not. I feel that only giving water to your Ancestors after they speak with you is more of a task-reward scenario. Again, we treat spirits, especially our own Ancestors, as we would if they had a physical body. WE NEVER TREAT THEM AS LESSER BEINGS. NEVER. I feel it is important to honor them regardless of how they choose to manifest. Some of the Ancestors will manifest very strongly and some will not. I do not reward or punish my Ancestors because they lack strength in their ability to manifest. A word of advice, we treat all spirits the way we would want to be treated when we have passed on and we become one of the Ancestors! I have heard of and seen other spiritual traditions that treat the Ancestors as children who misbehave and should be punished or rewarded. I never worry if an Ancestor will become powerful or not. Over time they will come into their power and strength. The more they work with you and the more energy you give the Ancestors by offerings and devotions, the more powerful they will become. You must be patient and loving. For my practice, I simply light my ancestral candle first, say the prayer, then pour water in each of the water bowls as I begin to talk to the Ancestors. If you follow this practice, you need to do this once a day until the energetic connection between you is strong and solid. The spirits understand that we humans become busy with our human affairs. We may not always have the time and energy to have long conversations. However, you should say a simple prayer every day. This helps them stay connected with you and feeds them energy.

Speaking with the Ancestors helps build the energetic bond between you. Speaking, singing, or chanting has the power to manifest magick. In many religions when God or the creator deities speak, the Universe is created. Likewise in magick, when we speak or sing with intention, we are bringing spirit down to the physical plane to manifest our will. When we talk with emotion and intention, the energetic bond between you and your Ancestors is strengthened. The more you speak to them, the more energy you give to them and, in turn, the more energy they give back to you. This also establishes an emotional relationship bond. Just as we must nurture our relationships with our friends and family, so too, we have to nurture our relationships with the dead. Our Ancestors have an investment in us because we are their family and their legacy. It is important to them to maintain family connections. They want to see us succeed. They want us to be happy and fulfilled in this plane of existence. The more powerful the family line is from this world to the spirit world, the more powerful the family influence is in all the worlds. Some of our Ancestors may not even know this, especially if they have not been in the Underworld for too long. However, our Ancestors who have been in the Underworld for generations have spiritually evolved to such a point that they are able to understand this concept and very much want to nurture this. These ancient Ancestors have their own mysteries that we may never come to understand in this life and plane of existence.

When you begin speaking with your Ancestors, at first you may not know what it is you should say or what the Ancestors would like to talk about. Typically, you can say anything you want. What do you think your Ancestors would be interested in? It is important to realize that they are your family. Your family is interested in what is going on in your life. To begin with, I would talk to them about what is happening to you day-to-day. You may speak with them about how work is going or about your romantic life if you feel that they are interested in that. Usually, grandmothers are interested in who we are dating and who are partners are. I think of speaking with the Ancestors as a magical phone call. I can light the ancestral altar candle, pour some water out to them, say my opening prayer, and then talk about my day, my hopes, fears, dreams, or anything that I think they want to hear about. There are no strict rules. However, if there are things you would not tell your Ancestors when they were alive, you may not want to talk about it when they are dead. I, personally, would not want to talk to my grandmother about my sex life while she was alive, so I would not do so during my conversations with her on the altar. As I said before, they will likely have the same worldviews and prejudices as they did when they were alive. However, they may slowly come around to new and strange ideas like magick, spirits, gay, and alternative lifestyles. They have a different perspective now and can see different sides of the energetic "coin." I will say that this sometimes takes a while, and you may have to be very patient with your Ancestors.

If, while working with your Ancestors, one of them refuses to accept things such as magick, working with the living, or does not approve of your lifestyle, it is important that you explain to them that if they cannot be accepting of you and your work, then you will take them off the altar and no longer give them offerings. Your Ancestors will soon see the energetic benefit of working with you and may have to change their views. But there have been several cases where a particularly stubborn family member would just rather be taken off the altar. This is completely fine. You should not change their destiny and spiritual evolution. You cannot rush spiritual transformation. Perhaps they will come back in time. It is always better to have a harmonious relationship with your Ancestors. One of the most common questions that is asked of me about the Ancestor Altar in the living room is: "Will Grandma and Grandpa see me having sex in the living room or my bedroom?"

This always makes me giggle, but it would be mortifying if they did! The truth of the matter is that whenever you do not want to be seen, your psychic mind automatically puts up a shield around you and whatever you are doing. On some level you want privacy, even if you are not consciously thinking about it and Poof! The shield goes up, cloaking your actions. This is true about your bedroom as well. Your bedroom is your sanctuary. Most people know never to go into someone's bedroom without permission and these same courtesies go for the Ancestors as well. However, just to be safe, I would not leave the candle on my Ancestor altar burning if I decide to become intimate with someone. Grandma may get a shock.

At times, some of your Ancestors may not work well together on the same altar. Sometimes, they take their stubbornness and disagreements into death with them. If your grandmother is very upset because Uncle Johnny stole a great deal of money from the family during life, she may take this anger into death with her. It is tedious, but you can play mediator between them. You may have to explain to them that what happened in life was a long time ago and they need to work on making amends, if not for their sake, then for the sake of the family and future generations. There have been family feuds and disagreements that have lasted so long no one really remembers how they got started. Even these can be resolved. If their minds are made up and they refuse to make amends after mediation, then you may want to consider taking one of them off the altar. When working with your Ancestors, you want the energy to be loving and focused. You do not want Uncle Joe's water dish being thrown off the altar. Yes, I have seen this happen!

After your conversation, say your goodbyes and extinguish the candle. You may use a candle extinguisher, or you may blow out the candle. Blowing out the candle is not disrespectful. It is the same as hanging up the telephone. When you are finished communing with your Ancestors, they may hang around a bit in your home or they may go back to whatever they were doing in the Afterlife before you called to them. I personally do not mind my Ancestors hanging around after the candle is blown out. Just as we said before, your Ancestors on your shrine are permanent residents in your home.

On special occasions, or whenever it feels correct, you may give them flowers and/or food. The kind of food is up to you. Generally, too much salt drains their energy so avoid salty foods and foods that have a lot of preservatives. You should also de-shell or peel food as needed. Give meat sparingly. There are many spiritual traditions that give meat and animal sacrifice to the Ancestors. I do not interfere with those traditions, but for myself I prefer to keep the meat to a minimum. I give them meat on special occasions and holidays. If they did not like a meal during life, they won't like it in death either. Alcohol is fine on holidays and birthdays, but drunken spirits are not always the easiest to control or calm down. If they had a drinking problem in life DO NOT GIVE ALCOHOL. There may be times when we did not realize that one of our Ancestors had a drinking or drug problem. A lot of the time the dead have the same addictions and problems after death. If you have an Ancestor who continually asks or demands alcohol outside of a special holiday treat you need to be firm with them and explain that you are not going to provide it for them and if they continue to ask for it, they will be taken off the altar. I do not like to threaten Ancestors any more than I like to threaten a human being, but we must remember that those spirits with drug and alcohol problems need you to be firm and loving.

How the Dead Appear

As you are doing your work with your Ancestors, you are building a psychic connection at the same time as developing your astral and spiritual sight. When you begin, you may feel like you are imagining the voices of your Ancestors. This is a good thing. The idea is not to "make up" the conversation in your head, but to just let it happen naturally. It may feel like you are making it up, but you are not. This takes practice so do not rush it. For some people it happens very quickly and for others it takes longer. This has nothing to do with how much psychic ability you may or may not have, but rather how strong your connection is with the spirits of the dead. When you have your conversations, give each Ancestor water in their bowl whether they spoke to you or not. It is not often that all your Ancestors will speak with you. Perhaps only one or two will speak, and often only one. When you feel it is appropriate, you can give food offerings to your Ancestors, and this will give them strength to manifest more easily on this plane of existence. When your psychic skills are improved and your Ancestors are stronger, it will be much easier to have conversations with them.

Once you begin having regular conversations with the dead, you may start to see them in your mind. This is a good indication that your connection to your Ancestors is becoming stronger. The vision in your mind may be hazy or fuzzy at first, but it will clear up in time. Often, after the Ancestors have been dead a while, they will appear as they did in the prime of their life. I often hear that they appear as the age of 33, but in my experience, they appear as the time in their lives when they were the healthiest and happiest. This happens because your consciousness has an immensely powerful effect on the astral and spiritual bodies. In energy healing, we teach that your thoughts have a direct effect on your energy bodies and your health. The same applies here. The spirit body will appear in the way that is the most pleasing to the spirit. In other words, if your grandmother died at 85 and had some debilitating disease at the time of death, she may very well appear later to you as a young and healthy woman. I have even seen adults appear as children. This is rare but it does happen.

After working with your Ancestors regularly for a time, you may no longer just see them in your mind. They may manifest in spirit right in front of you in your living room. If this happens, most likely they will all appear at the same time. I have never seen only one or two of my Ancestors appear while the others on my altar did not. At this stage of development, the only difference between your Ancestors and any other houseguest is that your Ancestors do not have a physical body. You may even see them roaming around your house! Do not worry, only you and other clairvoyants will be able to see them. They usually only appear before you when you light the candle on the ancestral altar and say a prayer to them. Once the candle is extinguished, they disappear. This does not mean that you have banished them, but you have temporally "turned off" the connection that brings them to the forefront of your consciousness. They are still there on the astral and spiritual planes.

Evolution and Transformation of the Dead

In many cultures around the world, it is common for the living to pray to and for the dead. This is done for a variety of reasons. Prayers are heard throughout all three worlds and on all levels of existence. When we pray, we are using energies from our minds, emotions, spirit, and in some instances, our bodies. It is interesting to note that in indigenous cultures it is often common to pray to the spirits through dance and ordeals such as the sweat lodge and Sundance Ceremony. The sweat lodge, or *inipi* in Lakota, is a ceremony where the seekers go into a small lodge or hut. There, water is poured over hot rocks making hot steam. During the ceremony, powerful spirits and the Ancestors are called into the lodge, and they are prayed to for healing. The Sundance is a four-day event where the seekers dance all day and pray to the spirits for a vision that will aid the people in the times to come. When we pray with reverence and heartfelt feelings, our prayers are made stronger and more powerful. This is not to say that people who "care" more get better results necessarily, but it does mean that if we do not put much feeling and energy into our prayers then they may or may not get to the party intended. I personally believe that our personal gods and Ancestors are with us all the time and they always hear our prayers, but the difference is that they can tell how much we mean it when we pray.

In Shinto, the Japanese indigenous animistic religion, it is believed that the Ancestors need to be purified after death so that they may transcend to higher levels of existence. The higher levels of existence are more refined. This means that spirits who dwell in the "higher" planes of existence need to be in harmony and balance with these energies to be able to exist there. The benefit of transitioning to a higher realm is that, once there, the spirit can evolve and transform on a deeper level. The Shinto belief is that when the Ancestors have achieved this level of transformation, they are better equipped to become teachers and spirit guides for their families and community.

As living beings, we can help our Ancestors to evolve and transform through our prayers. When we pray for the purification, teaching, and transformation of our Ancestors, there are certain helping and healing spirits that will hear our prayers and help them to evolve and transform into more than they were at the time of death. There are Divine Ancestors, those Ancestors who have reached a high level of transformation, perhaps even becoming gods themselves, who have a personal investment in their bloodline and who will be able to help the dead learn to transform into higher beings. There are also healing spirits who can help the Ancestors heal from past hurts and tragedies and even unfinished business that cause the Ancestors to hold onto things that prevent them from moving to a higher level of being. In Native American cultures there are the Holy Medicine People. These are spiritual beings of great power that are wise in the ways of healing and transcendence. It is believed that their divine purpose is to help humanity find balance to evolve and transform. They will help both the living and the dead find the spiritual teachings they need to find their divine purpose in life and in death. We pray to higher beings because both the living and the dead have free will. Enlightened beings will only help us and those we love if we ask for it. When the

Universe created life, it did so with the idea of Free Will. The Universe allows us to make our own successes and mistakes and will not interfere unless it is necessary. It is true that one of their purposes is to help us, but they cannot interfere with our decisions for good or for ill. They will respect the path that we are currently on and help in the limited ways that they are able until we ask them through our prayers.

Once we put our intent in motion of helping our Ancestors evolve, then the higher beings take the Ancestors to a place where they can be taught how to become higher beings themselves. When this happens, our Ancestors can become more powerful and enlightened. They are then able to help us on the physical plane in more profound ways. They may become spirits guides and act as "guardian angels" for us. They will be able to help our family and us in more profound and tangible ways. They will also be able to help other people in a way that is beneficial to everyone.

On an energetic level, what is happening is that our prayers open our mind, energies, emotions, and our spirits to our Ancestors and higher beings to establish a strong and powerful connection. Through the connection we make with the spirits, they can use this energy and power to help our Ancestors evolve to a higher state of being. This is done over time, so it is important that we pray to our Ancestors and higher beings every day. It is also important that we give our Ancestors water and food offerings from time to time so that they can maintain their energetic connection with this world. You will begin to see how the Ancestors manifest in the physical plane quite easily. However, it is important to remember that it does indeed take time. In the Underworld, there is no concept of time how we are used to thinking about it. The Ancestors literally have all the time they need. You cannot rush spiritual evolution. Some of our Ancestors may learn and evolve very quickly and other may take more time. There is no right or wrong way. It just is what it is. From our point of view, it may seem time consuming, but to our Ancestors point of view it may seem to be happening very quickly, or vice versa. The important thing to remember is to give your Ancestors the love and respect of being your family and your guides. After a while, this process will seem very natural to you and will become a part of your daily life.

Dreams with the Dead

Dreams are the gateway into the three worlds. Many pagan cultures, believe that the dream world is more "real" than the physical plane. One reason they believe this is because the dream world closely resonates with the spirit world. It has been in existence far longer than the physical plane and will be there long after the Earth, the physical universe, and all physical reality is long gone. The Dreamworld is a world or plane of its own, but it is also a portal or gateway into the Underworld. The gods, Ancestors, and nature spirits are able to easily communicate with us through our dreams. When the Ancestors come into our dreams we may ask the question, *are we dreaming of the Ancestors or are the Ancestors dreaming of us?* In dreams, things seem odd and magical. We can be in our homes and then instantly be across the world. In dreams, Ancestors can appear as they wish. Perhaps they appear as they did in life, but they can appear in any form they wish. The magick of dreams is closely related to the Underworld. In dreams we can certainly travel to the Underworld, but most often we are traveling in the Dreamworld itself.

    A safe and effective way to speak with your Ancestors and the dead is through the ritual of incubation. In necromancy, incubation refers to speaking with the dead through dreams. This is a relatively easy process and sometimes happens without our even realizing it. A benefit of dream incubation with the dead is that we are not inviting them into our space in the physical plane, but we are meeting them in an in-between place.

Before performing your Incubation Ritual, you will need to take a purifying bath or shower. You may add purifying essential oils to your bath such as peppermint, eucalyptus, lavender, or sage. You should also smudge your sleeping area with sage, sweet grass, frankincense, and/or lavender.

Ancestor Dream Ritual

1. Begin by creating sacred space. This can be a circle or simply a declaration to the spirits that your bed and bedroom is sacred and magical.

2. Say a prayer to your personal gods, asking them for guidance and protection. Then say a prayer to Persephone, Hella, Gwyn Ap Nudd, Osiris, or whichever Underworld god or goddess is most appropriate to your religious tradition, asking them to allow your Ancestors to speak with you. You can say something like this, "Hella, Goddess of the Underworld and of the Dead. I ask that you grant my Ancestors temporary leave of your kingdom so that I may learn from their insight."

3. Next say a prayer to Hermes, Hecate, Mercury, Cernunnos or whichever god or goddess of the crossroads, gates, or ghost roads is most appropriate to your religious tradition. It should be a deity who allows the dead to travel to the Earth plane from the Underworld. For example: "Great Hermes. You who travels the worlds. Grant my Ancestors safe passage to the world of dreams"

4. On your altar, or other sacred place in your home, lay out an offering in a bowl for the gods. The Greco-Roman deities I work

with like red wine, honey, beans, chickpeas, barley, and milk. You can also research other cultures to see what offering they left their gods. You can also use your intuition. Sometimes this is a particular deity speaking to you asking for something they especially like. If it feels right to leave out something other than what the sources tell you, then do so.

5. In a separate bowl, leave an offering to the Ancestors. You can choose water, milk, rice, bread, fruit, or whatever you feel is appropriate.

6. Then lie down. Just before you go to sleep make one last statement to the Otherworld. "I travel to the world of dreams so that I may speak with my Ancestors."

7. Allow yourself to drift off to sleep. Know that you will see your Ancestors in your dreams. Try not to have any preconceived notions about what will happen and how they will appear. Allow the dream to unfold. The Ancestors may appear as they did when they died, or they may appear younger and healthier. They may even appear in another guise. Don't worry, in the dream worlds you will know them instinctively. Sometimes they will appear as animals or simply an energy or fog. You may not immediately succeed or be aware of your success at first if you are not used to doing this sort of magical work. Do not become discouraged. Keep at it. Eventually, you will achieve success. This may range from a dramatic encounter in the Dreamtime, a curious gut feeling about something that you experience upon waking, or something that drifts into your consciousness over the course of the next day.

8. Upon awakening, thank your gods, the gods of the Underworld and the Gatekeepers, and your Ancestors. Even if you do not

remember your dreams, you must still thank all those spirits that you called upon.

9. Journal your experience. Write down impressions, thought, or insights. Sometimes when we perform the Ancestor Dream Ritual, we may not remember seeing our ancestors but they were there. In the beginning it may take a few attempts before we are able to see them clearly. Try to remember how you felt and what was happening. Maybe the Ancestors were observing you or maybe they were sharing energy with you without taking form. I try not to judge my dream experience. Journal what you can and try again the next night.

Exercise: Meditation on Being an Ancestor

I believe the relationship between a person and their Ancestors should be even stronger than their relationship with their gods. In an effort to better understand what it must be like for your Ancestors, I am providing a guided meditation that will allow you to have a better understanding on what it is like for your Ancestors. This is important because it helps us open or heart to them in a more compassionate way so that we can have a basic understanding on what it might be like for them. In this meditation, you will perform a guided visualization that will help you better understand the death experience. This is simply for you to better understand your Ancestors. You will not be harmed in any way.

Meditation:

Lie down and make yourself comfortable. Take a deep breath in and exhale the day's stress away. Take another deep breath in and allow the chatter in your mind to quiet. Take one more deep breath and release the tension in your muscles. Center yourself in your body.

You are in hospice hooked up to life support machines. You have lived a full life and now your body is weakening moment by moment. Your family and friends are at your side. There are tears in the room, but you are not sad. Your time has come to leave the physical plane and enter the spirit world. You will miss your family and friends, but you know that it is time for you to move on. The doctors have turned off the life support machines, and you can feel your body and life fading away. As this is happening you feel a strong spiritual presence all around you.

There are spirit helpers, spirit guides, and your Ancestors standing all around your bed. There is a sense of safety and mystery surrounding you. The machines have registered that your heart has stopped. Your life force is gone. You can feel your astral body separating from your physical body without effort. One of your Ancestors reaches out to you with their hand and helps your astral body off the bed.

A portal opens about the size of a door. There is a bright light coming from the magical doorway. Your Ancestors lead you through and your guides accompany you as well. You do not know what is on the other side of the door, but you know that it is the afterlife. After going through the door, you find yourself in a city. This is the land of the Ancestors. What does this place look like to you? Are the buildings large or small? Are they modern or old? Who is there when you get to the land of the Ancestors? Is there anyone here that you recognize? After a time, you start to become acclimated to this wonderful place. You meet Ancestors from your family lineage that go back thousands of years. You also meet friends and spiritual teachers who were once your companions in life. All family. All Ancestors.

Not too long after you have met your Ancestors in afterlife, you hear a spirit voice call your name. The voice is getting stronger and stronger, and it seems to pull you. It is almost as if your blood is dragging you back across the great spirit veil that separates you from the world of the living. You cannot resist the magical call. You follow the call through the veil. You find yourself standing in an unfamiliar living room next to an altar of some kind. You walk closer to examine the altar and you discover your picture on top of the table with a bowl of water for you. You look around and see a young person saying prayers for you. In a moment, other Ancestors appear, ones you recognize.

"She has called you!" One of your Ancestors says.

You look at the young person and you do not recognize them. Their clothes seem strange and not what you remember at all from life. You look around the living room and notice that the furniture seems odd, like something from a science fiction movie. You see a calendar on the wall and see the date. It is 60 years after you died.

After the young person finishes their prayers for you and the other Ancestors, they pour water in the bowls on the altar. "Drink it," an Ancestor says.

You take a drink of the water placed in front of your picture. You feel refreshed and powerful. You feel a strong connection to the young person. Without asking them and without anyone telling you, you know their name. You've always known their name. You feel an incredible bond with them. You will do anything for them. You will open the gates of the spirit world for them. You will protect them. What they ask of you, you will do…out of love. They are your family. You are their Ancestor.

Trickster Spirits and Negative Entities

Occasionally you may attract spirits who are not your Ancestors. Most of the time these are spirits who have noticed your work with the dead and pass by because of curiosity or would like to ask your help in some way. You are not obligated to help them. For me, this is a part of my spiritual work so if I am able, and my spirits advise me that it is right, and then I will help in whatever way I can.

Sometimes, entities or negative spirits may not have the best intentions in mind. Most of the time these spirits are looking to consume the energy that you are providing to your Ancestors. It is not a good idea to allow this to happen. It is very probable that the spirit will become stronger and more manipulative to obtain the energy and power it desires. It is better to deal with it before it becomes too powerful.

To deal with trickster spirits, the easiest thing to do is to touch your ancestral altar and call upon your spirits. Explain to them the situation (trust me when I say they already know!) and ask them to get rid of the spirit. Then visualize you and your ancestors making a circle holding hands while you are physically touching the altar. Visualize a brilliant white light that is purifying surround you, your Ancestors, and the altar. Know that this light is sending the trickster spirit far away and to another entity or god that may help this entity on its spiritual path. As you perform this little ritual, make sure you are doing it in a way that is compassionate and healing. We are not aiming to harm the trickster spirit, simply send it to another being who is able to give the spirit the healing it needs.

If you should encounter tricksters or negative entities, do not panic. Most of these beings are simply lost or confused and know that the energy you are providing for your Ancestors can give them "life" and nourishment. Just as stated above, they are easily persuaded to leave. Occasionally, you may have an entity that attaches itself to you and drains your life force. The best way to prevent this is to make sure you have healthy dietary habits, exercise regularly, solid spiritual beliefs, and practices that include devotional work. If you do manage to acquire a spiritual attachment, there are a few things you can do to remove the entity.

1. You or a friend can take a consecrated knife or dagger and cut the

spirit away. Visualize a cord between you and the spirit and see the knife cutting the cord. If the spirit is still there, refer to the "Banishing" techniques described later in the book to banish the spirit. This is the most aggressive of the techniques and should only be done when the others do not work.

2. You can take a bath in salt water. Salt drains the energy of spirits and they will quickly go away. I like to think of it as like putting salt on a slug to kill it.

3. Ask your gods and goddesses to remove the spirit. You can light a candle to them and send them a prayer asking them to take the spirit to a place of healing. Then visualize your god or goddess coming to remove the spirit and taking it away.

4. Ask your healing helpers, holy medicine people, and divine Ancestors to come and remove the spirit from you and take it to a place of healing.

You may use any of the above techniques that suit you or you may use a combination of them.

Finding an Ancestral Teacher

While working with the dead and your Ancestors, you will need to be able to maneuver through the Underworld. One of the best ways to accomplish this is to find your Ancestral Teacher. This is a distant Ancestor who has evolved spiritually to an advanced level and has chosen to remain in the Underworld to watch and guide your family line. This teacher no longer has the need of things associated with the physical plan, yet still retains the memories of life and understands what it is to be human. Your Ancestral Teacher has many abilities that they can teach you to work more effectively with the Ancestors and the dead. One of the most important things is that they can teach you is how to better navigate the Underworld. There are places that the novice Underworld traveler should avoid until they are better prepared. It is not necessarily that we wish to avoid frightening and dangerous places, but also that there are certain strange realms that it is important to know and understand the customs that belong to that world. For example, if you find yourself in Svartalfheim, the land of dwarves and dark elves, you might find yourself in a jam because Dark Elves rarely make friends with outsiders, and they prefer to be left alone. Because of this, it is best to avoid them and leave them on their own or you may find yourself betrayed for your imposition. The Ancestral Teacher will help better prepare you for what is to come when you encounter such entities.

Your Ancestral Teacher has been watching your family for a long time and has spent years spiritually guiding your family throughout the generations. This teacher can assist you in your spiritual development when it comes to the dead and the Underworld. Whenever you have questions about your family lineage, your teacher is the best one to go to for advice. Your Ancestral Teacher can also assist you in learning Underworld divination and how to advance your magical experience using the ancestral and Underworld energies.

To Find Your Ancestral Teacher:

1. Sit in a comfortable chair or lie down. Relax your body and clear your mind. Begin to breathe slowly and connect yourself with the universal energies.

2. Visualize a Great Tree in front of you. It is the most magnificent and magical tree you have ever seen. You know this is the World Tree and will take you to anywhere in the three worlds you wish to go.

3. State your intention to find your Ancestral Teacher.

4. Your spirit animal greets you at the tree. You will both journey forth together. You see a door in the trunk of the tree. You open the door and see that there is a spiral staircase that seems to go down forever. Using your astral body, quickly move down the spiral staircase until you find the very bottom deep in the roots of the Tree.

5. As you step out of the tree's roots, you find yourself in the Underworld. What do you see? What can you hear? Smell?

6. Again, state your intention to find your Ancestral Teacher. The blood in your veins begins to vibrate. It seems as though your blood is guiding you now. Your spirit animal will guide you to your Ancestral Teacher.

7. As you journey forth, take notice of the landscape. What does it look like? Are you in a forest, desert, or prairie? Are you in a town or a city?

8. After a time, you find your Ancestral Teacher. Your teacher will make themselves known to you. You know this is your Ancestral Teacher because your blood vibrates stronger now in your astral body and you feel a family bond with this teacher. What does your teacher look like?

9. Spend some time asking your Ancestral Teacher questions and get to know them. When you are ready to leave say your goodbyes and journey back the way you came. Go back to the root of the tree, go up the spiral staircase and make your way back to the Midworld.

10. When you are ready open your eyes. Journal about your experience.
    Ancestral Patterns

Our family history is in our DNA. That which is spiritual manifests on the physical and that which is physical manifests on the spiritual. Our family passes physical attributes down to us. Likewise, they pass spiritual influences and karma. That is not to say that their religious beliefs are necessarily part of our genetic makeup, but rather that they pass down energetic patterns and unfinished business as well as blessings and curses.

We may notice patterns throughout our entire family. Sometimes these patterns go back to our grandparents, but other times these patterns go back for generations. We have the ability to change and alter these patterns and energies forever. We have the power to make a difference in our family lineage.

It is important to remember that this is not about blame or resentment. We have to understand that our Ancestors come from a completely different time and environment than we live in today. Most people simply were doing the best they could with what resources they had. They were human just like us. They made mistakes, had prejudices, hopes, fears, and disappointments just like we do now. To learn to clear ancestral patterns and karma, we need to have compassion. In fact, if you do not have the utmost compassion for your Ancestors then this work is not for you. Period.

Astral Traveling to Experience the Ancestors

This technique will help you learn more about the lives and history about your Ancestors. The purpose is to simply observe. Do not attempt to manifest yourself or make yourself known to your Ancestors or manipulate them in any way. Remember that in this exercise you are an observer. You are observing an energetic "echo" of lives that once were.

1. Lie down and find a comfortable position. Close your eyes and

relax as much as possible. Take a few deep breaths and release the tension in your body.

2. Visualize an energetic cord extending from your navel chakra. As it implies, this is the energetic center just below your navel. I see this cord as a blood red (blood/Ancestors), but you may see this cord as any color that feels appropriate. Know that this cord is of your blood and DNA and leads back to your Ancestors. You may also see the cord coming from the heart chakra if this works better for you. Bring your conscious awareness to the chord. From your point of view, the chord looks like a great tunnel that leads to your Ancestors.

3. Travel up this cord with your mind to your father. It does not matter if they are living or dead. You may use this technique in either case. See life through his eyes. When you are ready, come back to your body.

4. Travel up this cord with your mind to your mother. See her life through her eyes.

5. Now, pick either your mother or father and travel up the cord to your grandmother or grandfather. It doesn't matter which one. Just pick one at a time and experience his or her life through his or her eyes.

6. You may use your family tree to see what it was like to live in the world and time of that Ancestor. You do not need to know the names of your Ancestors in order to travel back and observe.

With this technique you will have a better understanding of what happened in the lives of your Ancestors and the feelings and energies surrounding them. When we have empathy for our Ancestors, we will have a stronger emotional bond with them. This bond will make your magick and Ancestor work rewarding.

Traveling to the Ancestors to Release Ancestral Patterns

This technique is similar to the previous technique, but this time your intent is to find ancestral patterns that are affecting your life. These may be mental, emotional, spiritual, or physical patterns and ailments.

1. Lie down and find a comfortable position. Close your eyes and relax as much as possible. Take a few deep breaths and release the tension in your body.

2. Visualize an energetic cord coming from your navel chakra. I see this cord as blood red (blood/Ancestors), but you may see this cord as any color that feels appropriate. Know that this cord is of your blood and DNA and leads back to your Ancestors.

3. Call upon your Spirit Animal and Ancestral Teacher. Ask them to journey with you and guide you to the Ancestor and the point in their life that caused the negative ancestral patterns.

4. With your Spirit Animal and Ancestral Teacher, travel forth into the Ancestral cord. Set the intent of finding the negative ancestral patterns. Use your intuition to decide if it stems from your father's side or mother's side. Then use your intuition again to decide if it's on your grandmother's side or grandfather's side, and so forth.

5. Many times, you will only have to go back a few generations, but at times you may have to travel back several generations. Use the guidance and advice of your Ancestral Teacher. If you are stumped and do not know which Ancestor to try, then you must try everyone! This can be time-consuming, but you will learn about your

family history and have a better understanding of your lineage.

6. Once you discover which Ancestor and event caused the negative pattern, it is at this point that you call upon your patron god and/or goddess to aid you in healing the energetic cord and the Ancestor. In the case of hate and jealousy, for instance, ask the gods to help your Ancestor to ease their pain. You may help them further by using basic energy work. You can do this by visualizing the negative pattern, emotion, or event turning into light and evaporating away from your cord and into the cosmos to be transmuted into something more constructive.

Make sure you are sending healing energy to the Ancestral cord and the Ancestors it directly pertains to. See this healing energy flow down into the Ancestral cord healing their offspring and then the next generation and then next until it comes to you.

NOTE: The perspective of the person and the events taking place may vary. You may be watching it like a play or movie; you could see it from a bird's eye view, or you may experience it from one of your Ancestors' point of view.

Family Karma

There may be family karma that has been carried down from generation to generation to you. You may have heard the rumors of the curses of the Kennedy family and the House of Windsor. Sometimes the actions of our Ancestors have created an energy rift or echo that travels down to us. Not all family karma has to do with devastation, murder, and chaos. It can be something more along the lines of angering a spirit or god. It could also be a lesson that your Ancestors must understand before they can evolve to the next level of their development.

You may use the above technique to find the karma on your ancestral line. Once you find it, you must ask the gods, Ancestors, and teachers you are working with what needs to be done on this plane and this time to rectify the situation. It may be as easy as giving offerings and prayers to a god or spirit. But it may be more difficult, and you may not be able to resolve the situation completely in this lifetime. Then again, you may. The best thing to do is listen to your gods, Ancestors, and spirits. They would never ask you to do anything dangerous and foolish. They will never tell you to kill yourself, or give away all your Earthly possessions, or do something illegal. If a spirit mentions this, you must banish them immediately without hesitation. Ask your Ancestors on your altar to help you do this.

If you agree to the advice the gods and Ancestors give you, then you must carry it out. If it is a donation to an organization then do it. If it is prayers and offerings to a spirit or god, then do it! It may take weeks or even years to heal the karma, but it must be done. If not by you, then the next generation of your magical lineage.

Performing Tasks for Ancestors

While working with the Ancestors, there may be times when they ask you to do tasks for them. It is completely up to you if this is something you would like to do to strengthen your bond with them. It is not a good idea to promise them something without hearing what it is they would like you to do first. Most of the time they will ask you to tell them how your family is doing. Yes, they can find out for themselves, but remember that your Ancestors love to sit and talk about Aunt So-and-So or gossip about Great Great Uncle So-and-So. Don't forget the tea and cookies when you do this! They may also ask for a favorite food or drink. There is no harm in this, and it will be a lovely treat for them if you do so. There may be times when they ask you to perform a task that is more difficult. For example, they may ask you to perform a task like obtain mementoes or pictures from their life. For some this is easy, for others it can be more of a challenge. Other times, they may ask you to obtain some object or do something that is virtually impossible, such as find the vase they once owned in 1754. Remember, time in the Underworld is different so they may have a hard time understanding that their vase has long since been destroyed. When something like this happens, explain the situation to the best of your ability.

Magick with Ancestors

Once you have a strong working relationship with your Ancestors you can ask for their aid in various types of magick. In the beginning of your relationship with your Ancestors you will need to build up their energy and trust. Unless the Ancestors you are working with on your altar are pagan or magical in some way, it will take a little bit of time before they are ready to work magick with you. Most likely, your Ancestors had little direct contact with the physical plane for some time. They may have observed you and your family, but that was probably the extent of it. Now, you are going to work with them in a very direct and powerful way. It will take time for you to build up their energy for them to influence the physical plane. The best way to do this is to continue to say your prayers to them, give them water every day, and offerings of food when you think it appropriate—such as holidays, sabbats, birthdays, and deathdays.

You will also want to increase their magical knowledge. You could teach them energy work and magick just as you would any student, but I prefer to let them learn at their own pace and in their own time. We do not honor the Ancestors because we want them to do things for us. We honor them because it shows them love and it strengthens our energetic ties to our past, present, and future. When they are strong enough to influence the physical world, it is just an added bonus. When you are meditating, working with the gods, or doing magick of any kind, invite the Ancestors into your ritual space and ask them to observe. They have the ability to see the ebb and flows of the energies that you are using better than you can. They will be able to see the matrix of how it works and why, so do not be surprised if they learn very quickly. Every little or large work of magick I do or any healing I do, I invite the Ancestors into my ritual space. I also answer any questions they might have. If you have an Ancestor that is angry that you are doing "witchcraft" explain to them the mechanics of energy work and magick and why you do what you do. If they still protest take them off the Ancestral altar. I have had colleagues that did this, and the Ancestor suddenly became more tolerant and open-minded once they found out they were not getting any more offerings.

When you notice that your Ancestors are more visible during rituals you may see that they are helping with healings, giving your spells energy, and helping you open portals and gates to the three worlds. Do not force them to do this or get upset if they are not learning as quickly as you would like. Let them go at their own pace. Just as any student of energy work and magick has strengths and weaknesses, so will your Ancestors. Some may enjoy divination with tarot and runes, whereas the rest may not. Some Ancestors may enjoy spell casting and ceremonial magick, and there are some Ancestors who may simply lend energy to whatever task you are doing. All these things are powerful blessings. Having your Ancestors present in ritual space is a special gift.

Eventually, your Ancestors will get to a place where you can petition them for magical work or aid. Almost all pagan and tribal cultures in history have practiced Ancestor petitioning. The thought here is that because our Ancestors have an invested interest in our wellbeing and happiness, they will do whatever is in their power and ability to help us, even more so than the gods. Ancestor petitioning is simply asking the Ancestors to help you obtain or accomplish something. Often, the Ancestors will be proficient in giving you advice whether you want it or not. But when they obtain skill and magical power, they are able to influence the physical world from the Underworld. To petition your Ancestors, light a candle on your ancestral altar and say a prayer for them. Then, place your hands on the altar and tell them of your day and what is going on. Next, explain the situation that you would like their help with and explain to them what you would like the outcome to be. When you are finished, give them offerings of water and food. Keep in mind that the Ancestors have the ability to see into the future better than you can. If your desired goal will cause you spiritual, emotional, or physical harm they most likely will not help you in that desire. This is not to say they will hinder any magick you may do for it, but they will not help their loved one cause themselves any harm.

Working with your Ancestors in magick is such a wonderful blessing. My rituals do not feel whole, balanced, and grounded until I call my Ancestors into the space. I truly feel your magick will feel more powerful and inspiring with their presence.

Calling Ancestors in Ritual

The Ancestors are a part of my everyday life. Not only do I light the candle on their altar and speak with them, but I also invite them to be with me in my everyday life. I may not always see them, but I know that they are there. They are my spirit guides in the truest sense of the word. We have talked about how the Ancestors have a vested interest in you because you are their blood and their future. They want you to succeed and become more evolved spiritually. The bond between you and your

Ancestors is strong and will remain as such for all eternity. I have found that asking your Ancestors to attend and aid you in ritual and magick is immensely powerful. Ancient pagans made it part of their spiritual practice to call upon the Ancestors. Native American, African tribal religions, Celtic, Hindu, and many other religions call upon the Ancestors in ritual.

As we have discussed, not all our Ancestors may have been magical when they were alive. However, they can learn magick easily since they no longer have a physical body and are able to see the energies at work in the Underworld. They can see the comings and goings of time and space and can see how magick and energy work are able to manifest in all the worlds. When first working with the Ancestors, you may find that they may have their own fears and prejudices of magick and may not understand why you are working with such energies. How I taught my Ancestors about magick was to invite them to observe my daily magical practices, prayers, and energy work. I did not force or even ask them to do any magick at first, but simply invited them into the ritual space to observe.

The Ancestors love it when you light your altar candle, pray for them, fill their bowls with water, and invite them to watch the different aspects of your life. They feel included in your life and a part of the family again. Remember, you may be the only living family member who speaks and works with them directly, so they will be naturally curious about your daily comings and goings. To begin with, I invited them to watch the daily practice of my energy work which included techniques from the Kabbalistic Lesser Banishing Ritual of the Pentagram. My grandfather, who grew up Jewish, recognized the names of God and found that ritual particularly interesting. My Ancestors seemed to be very fond of the energy healing work I did. After a couple of years of observation, learning magick through me, and their own spiritual evolution, they began to learn how to contribute to my magick in their own way. At first it was only a little bit, but after a time, it became more and more profound and powerful. The Ancestors have a great amount of access to the magick and energies from the Underworld and it can be used for powerful ends.

I never ever force my Ancestors or the dead in general to aid me in magick. I feel that this is completely unethical and an abuse of power. You would not like spirits forcing you to help them if you did not want to, so you should give them the same courtesy. Most of the time, the Ancestors will want to help you in your magick, so forcing them to do so is not necessary. So, what if they decide they do not want to help you in ritual and magick for whatever reason? If this turns out to be the case, then you should still honor them on your altar as members of your Ancestral family. You should let them know that you will be seeking out another Ancestor who is willing to work magick with you. If they are upset, then perhaps you need to have a conversation with them about remaining on the ancestral altar. Magick, ritual, and energy work is a part of your life, and you should never change your ideals and beliefs because your family, living or dead, wants you to.

The most powerful and spiritual magick you can do is through the Ancestors. They can help you do many things such as divination and helping you influence your fate. Above all, they are your family in spirit. They care for you even more than the gods do. You are everything they worked for during their life. You are the fruit of their labors and hard work. Even though they can become powerful spiritual allies, they are still flawed. Even though they are in spirit, they are still human. It is true that over time they will evolve spiritually, but they will still make mistakes and defiantly have their own opinion. My grandparents on my father's side are on my Ancestral Altar. My grandmother will ask me many questions about my life and the lives of my brothers—and have an opinion about it. She will often protest when I make a choice she does not like. She will tell me stories beginning with, "In my day…" At first, I would look at this like a cute things grandma says. Now, I see it as wisdom beyond the ages wrapped up in a tiny German lady who was able to take care of her family and teach her son how to take care of his and so forth. This is magick. This is why we light our candles.

4
Necromancy

Baldur's Dreams (Norse)

Baldur, the Norse god of beauty, wisdom, and light, began to have horrible dreams of shadows, skulls, and death. He dreamed of dark things in the night that were threatening him. He dreamed of monsters that told him stories of the darkness. The blackest darkness seemed to cover him. He dreamed that all would be lost and that he would die. Odin was told of these horrible dreams. He feared that perhaps his beautiful son, the blameless one, the most bright, dreamed of the future. Odin wasted no time. He mounted his eight-legged horse, Sleipnir, and traveled down to Hel. It is there he would find his answers.

In Hel, he rode over the dark bridge that led to the gates of the dead and past the dreaded hellhound that guarded the way. Odin's son was in danger. He must act quickly! As he rode, he noticed that the Realm of the Dead was decorated in gold. It seemed they were expecting someone of great importance. At the eastern gates of Hel, Odin found the burial mound of a great seeress. The All-Father used his magical charms and summoned her from her grave. The seeress was forced to obey the magick. She appeared before Odin.

Odin asked the seeress why Helheim was decorated in gold. The seeress was unhappy about being summoned from her grave. She explained to the Great God that Baldur would be taken down to the depths of Hel. She wanted desperately to return to her slumber. With magick, Odin forced her to stay. The desperate father of Baldur wanted only to save his son. The seeress told him that his own son, the blind Hod, would kill Baldur. Odin further questioned her about who would avenge his son's death and how the tragedy would come to pass. The seeress spoke of oaths of brothers who avenged their siblings and women who howled during the time of the mourning of Baldur. She then returned to her grave with the strange warning that she would never return again until Loki escaped from his bonds.

Necromancy

Necromancy is an ancient magical art of summoning the dead and working with them for a variety of reasons. Originally, Necromancy was a means of divining the future. Necromancy means divination of the dead. *Necro* means "dead" and *mancy* means "divination". During the Middle Ages and the Christian uprising, to use magick was considered evil and to summon the dead was even worse. The clerics taught that the magician was not calling the dead, they were really calling demons from hell. *Necromancer* came to be a common name for an evil witch or dark magician. We know through researching ancient cultures that this is not the case. Necromancy is a way that magicians could work with the dead and the Ancestors in a profound spiritual way.

As we remember, communion with the dead goes back to when the Shamans sought their help for the tribal community. The dead were the respected Ancestors of the tribe who wanted to aid the living. The honored dead protected the tribe from evil spirits, gave advice to the leaders, and divined the future for the tribe. The Ancestors were consulted to foretell of the winters to come, enemies that were planning attacks, and where to find food. Summoning the dead was important to the survival of the tribe. As the tribes progressed into cities, the use of the Ancestors progressed as well. The Shaman summoning the dead for the tribe became the magician summoning the dead for political reasons and even for the common person seeking the aide of the spirits.

Reasons for Summoning the Dead

Working with the dead was a very sacred and spiritual act. The Necromancers who specialized in this art knew to treat the dead with great respect, and they only utilized this art so when it was thought necessary. There were many reasons to summon the dead. One of the most common reasons was to get advice from the spirit in question. It was thought that the spirits of the dead could see things that the living could not. They also retained the talents and wisdom that they once had in life. Therefore, it was common practice to go to the burial place of a king to get advice on matters of the kingdom and the land. You could also summon the spirit of a poet or bard to gain understanding of song and lyric. Another reason the dead were summoned was to gain power from the Underworld. As we have seen, there is much wisdom and magical treasure to be found in the Underworld. The dead had the ability to help you find these places of power. Also, the dead were summoned for works of divination. Just as stated before, the dead could see things come to be in the Underworld before they manifested in the physical world. They had firsthand knowledge concerning things that were soon to come.

Sacred Places

To summon the dead, the magician or necromancer needed to find those sacred places that were gateways or entrances into the Realm of the Dead. Entrances and gateways were places or objects that became a catalyst for the dead to manifest, or a part of this world that seemed to blend into the Underworld. The most common places to summon the dead were graves and gravestones. Some believed that a part of the soul remained near the body after death and could easily be summoned there. Others believed that the grave or bones of the dead acted as a "doorway" to the Underworld. I personally have found that the grave/bones of the dead act as a signature or magical DNA. Meaning that the DNA of someone never changes and can act as the magical "phone number" to get into contact with that person. If we take a look at how our DNA works, it is the building blocks of our human bodies and ancestral lineage. Even though we share our DNA with our ancestors, part of our DNA is uniquely ours. No one on earth or the spirit worlds has DNA exactly like ours. Even DNA between twins is somewhat different. Because of this the bones and remnants of our bodies can be used to "tune" into us after death.

Lakes were thought to be entrances into the Underworld much like the sea. The lakes seemed to go deep under the Earth and to the ancients it made sense that the lake led to the Realm of the Dead. Burrows in the ground were thought to have a similar function. I often think of *Alice in Wonderland* and how the rabbit hole led to a magical land. Mounds were thought to be the Underworld rising up to greet this world. Sometimes these mounds are referred to as "Faerie Mounds." I have often been asked if Faerie Mounds and Burial mounds are one and the same. I think the answer can be yes and no. I believe that natural hills or mounds are an access port to the Underworld. They do not necessarily have to take you to the land of the dead, but they certainly can. Remember, the Underworld has its own laws and rules and as soon as we think we have figured it out we learn quickly that there is always more to learn. Then there are forests that are dark and very ancient. Of course, this would be a perfect place to summon the dead because of the feeling of darkness and death that might be nearby. The darkness of the forest was very foreboding to the ancient people who believed that monsters lurked deep within. Danger could be lurking all about in the form of wild animals, thieves, and murderers. It was also secluded; and necromancers knew that most people would stay far from the dreaded dark forest because of the very thing they were about to do.

Sacred Times

Magical timing was also important to Necromancers. There were certain times of the month and year that were better suited for the practice of calling up the dead. The phases of the moon, sun, and stars could amplify the power needed for summoning. The dark and full moon were ideal for this purpose. Each had a special advantage over the other. The full moon has a powerful effect on magick. The energy emitted by the full moon helps the spirits to become more visible to the magician. During this time of the month, it was common to summon the dead for wisdom, advice, and power. The dark moon has its secrets as well. During this time, works of a darker nature were undertaken, such as binding spirits, divination, and summoning spirits to attack enemies.

There were certain times of the year that were especially powerful for calling forth the dead. The Celtic Fire Festival of Samhain, which happens around November 1, is thought to be the most powerful time of year for spirit work. Samhain is the Celtic holy day that begins the dark half of the year on or around October 31 in the modern calendar. At this time of year, the weather turns cold and the last of the crops is harvested. The Celts could see the power of decay and death all around them. The winds howled and the land around them seemed to die. Naturally, they thought that if the land was dying then it was turning into a sort of "land of the dead" and it would be easier to call upon the dead for works of magick.

Another powerful time was Yule. This holiday comes from the Nordic peoples and is another name for the time around the Winter Solstice, December 21. Traditionally, the Celts did not celebrate the solstices and equinoxes, only the events that fell in-between these days. It was not until much later that the solstices and equinoxes were observed. Nevertheless, to the Northern European people this was a powerful time for calling the dead. Yule is the longest night of the year. The world around these ancient people was barren and most likely frozen over. The Land of the Dead was truly upon them, and the dead could surely be found in the woods or in some forbidding corner of the landscape. The energy was perfect for calling forth the dead.

Cemeteries

To me, cemeteries have always had a holy and sacred feel to them, as well as a sense of Otherworldliness. When we visit cemeteries during the day, the grounds feel like they are holy and protected by higher spirits. However, after dark, cemeteries may have a strange and sometimes foreboding energy to them. This is not because the spirits are most active at night. The spirits are active all the time, we are just aware of them mostly at night. During the day, the sun emits a very large amount of ion into the atmosphere. This solar energy can drown out the spirits astral and spiritual bodies. At night, we are able to see and feel the spirits more clearly because the moon only emits a small amount of ion and the spirits can be easily seen. This is not to say that you cannot see spirits during the day. You certainly can. It just takes more psychic ability to do so. The grounds, themselves, are usually blessed by a local priest or rabbi so that no lower energetic beings will bother the spirits that are laid to rest there. Cemeteries were first built for several reasons. One reason was to keep the dead bodies away from the living. When a corpse is decomposing, it releases toxins into the ground. Those toxins can sometimes make their way into the drinking water of nearby people. Another reason was to keep the dead bodies close to the church or temple so that they would be spiritually safeguarded from negative spirits and from grave robbers.

Some belief systems say that the spirits of the dead stayed close by their graves and that a necromancer could easily summon a spirit by going to their grave. One reason for this is because to effectively summon the dead, you need to know their name. In modern times, the name of the deceased is often placed upon the grave marker. Another reason is that when the necromancer is close to the remains of the deceased it is easier to summon the spirit because there is an energetic imprint on the remains that link them to the spirit. In my belief, a spirit does not actually remain in the graveyard unless it chooses to. But when summoned, the grave acts as a portal that can easily summon the spirit back to its remains.

There are several stories and legends about the ghosts of the dead that haunt graveyards for a myriad of reasons. One can pick up any horror novel or movie and find such a story. The spirits of the dead have other business to attend to and do not "haunt" graveyards unless there is a particularly good reason.

Cemeteries do a have a spirit Gatekeeper. The Gatekeeper is a spirit that can be found close by the actual gate of the cemetery or sometimes in the very center of it. The duty of the Gatekeeper is to keep away unwanted energies, people, and spirits who wish to harm or desecrate the graves in some way. When a magician wishes to work with the spirits in the cemetery it is wise to ask the permission of the Gatekeeper. To do this, you simply use your intuition to find the Gatekeeper. They can be found in a statue, a tree, or some other object. Then you can ask for their permission to allow you to do your work. The Gatekeeper may or may not speak to you directly. Gatekeepers vibrate on a higher level and do not always speak in the ways we are used to. I allow my intuition to guide me. When asking the Gatekeeper's permission, you will feel if it is correct to go further with your work. If it feels correct, continue. If not, pay your respects to the Gatekeeper and try again another day. There may be several reasons why the Gatekeeper barred your way into the Cemetery. Perhaps there are several people visiting relatives that day and they would disturb your work. Or perhaps the spirits are unwilling to be bothered. Know that the Gatekeeper has the best interest of the spirits in the cemetery and will always be looking out for them. You do not always know what is happening energetically in the cemetery and you must trust that the Gatekeeper knows what is best.

When I am in the cemetery, the ground feels sacred and magical. It literally feels like I am in a sanctuary. However, you may find that if you dig up a little dirt and take it beyond the borders of the cemetery, the energy of the dirt changes. It may seem to become infused with the energy of death and decay. There are several Hoodoo spells that require graveyard dirt for magick and cursing. Some of those spells are intended to harm and even kill its target. I have to laugh when I see graveyard dirt "substitute." There is no such thing. Graveyard dirt is graveyard dirt and there is no substitute. It just does not exist. If you choose to dig up graveyard dirt in the cemetery, you must remember a couple of rules: First, ask the spirits before you go digging up their sanctuary. To do so without permission is very disrespectful and you may get an energetic slap in the face. I would not chance that. Second, leave money or coins where you dig up the dirt. Believe it or not, the dead do like money. Remember, the ferryman Charon requires payment before he will carry the spirits of the dead across the river Styx. There are other rules, each according to the custom of the religious beliefs of the dead and that of the magician. Just because you do not know the customs does not mean that the spirits will not hold you accountable.

When working rituals and magick in the cemetery there is also a chance that spirits will follow you home. I have heard of magicians that say that you must walk backwards out of a cemetery and all the way home so that a spirit will not follow you back. If you live several miles from a graveyard then this will be tricky indeed. I do not personally feel that this is necessary. If you pay respects to the Gatekeeper going in and out of the cemetery and are respectful to the sanctuary and the spirits within, you should be fine. However, sometimes a spirit may still follow you out. When this happens, there are a couple of choices. You may ask the spirit what it wants from you and decide if you are able and willing to help it. You could banish the spirit. You could also put the spirit back into the graveyard and allow the Gatekeeper to take care of it. Sometimes the spirit will attach itself to you with an energetic cord or simply latch on to you. If that is the case, I see no harm in coming to an agreement with the spirit. It may ask for offerings of food and water to aid you. It may need your assistance with a task. Ask the spirit what the task is and decide if you are able and willing to perform the task. If you are able to perform the task and you agree to it make sure you do what the spirit asks in a reasonable amount of time, otherwise the spirit may become upset and cause havoc in your home. It is best to negotiate the timeframe with the spirit at the moment you make this contract. If you cannot help the spirit for whatever reason, then explain this to the spirit and ask your gods and Ancestors to help the spirit find a magician who can.

If the spirit is hostile to you and your home and will not leave, then you must banish it. There are several ways to banish a sprit, and these will be discussed later in this book.

Mausoleums

When you tour a cemetery, you may find two types of mausoleums. One type of mausoleums are the small structures that house caskets. It can house a single casket, or it can house a whole family of caskets. They come in a variety of shapes and sizes. I am sure they were inspired by the Egyptian pyramids and the Northern European grave mounds. The purpose of mausoleums, in a mundane sense, is for the family of the deceased to be able to visit the caskets above ground. In large cemeteries, you may find many mausoleums in a variety of styles. The more lavish mausoleums usually belong to well-to-do families.

The magician can use the mausoleums as portals into different times and dimensions. It is a useful magical technique that the advanced magician can utilize during his work with the Ancestors and the dead. I have been transported back in time to whence the mausoleums were created or to when that family was alive and well. Very rarely will you come across a mausoleum that was specifically designed and created for magick. It happens seldom, but it does happen. Living in Chicago, I have been fortunate enough to come across such mausoleums several times. The best way to find these special portals is, of course, energetically. They seem to hum with an energy that is waiting to be used for magick. Another way to tell if the mausoleum was intended for magick is to look at the design of the structure. You may find magical symbols engraved on the structure and statues of gods, goddesses, spirits, and other magical beings. If you find such a mausoleum count yourself lucky. A magician may use any mausoleum for magick; however, some are energetically stronger than others.

To use the mausoleum for magick you must first speak with the spirits on the inside of the mausoleum. There may be a family guardian spirit around the entrance. If so, remember to state who you are and what your intentions are with the mausoleum and the spirits who dwell inside. The guardian of the mausoleum will be able to tell from your energy if you mean well or not. If the guardian spirit accepts your intentions, there are a couple of options you may have to work with the structure. You may touch the door of the mausoleum and astrally project yourself going through the door. The door may be a portal in itself or you may simply go inside. If you do not wish to physically place your hands on the door you do not have to. I find that it provides a stronger connection. However, some magicians feel that by touching the mausoleum they are invading the space of the family of spirits inside. I personally feel that if you clearly explain your intentions to the guardian spirit and you have permission to use the structure as a portal, then you also have permission to touch the building. Once you are astrally inside the mausoleum, you may see other portals and doors to other places. Feel free to explore them all. They may take you to different times and dimensions or ever alternate universes. All these can provide you with opportunities to learn and grow spiritually.

If a family guardian does not give you permission to be inside, respect the wishes of the family and find another mausoleum. Never magically force your way in. Doing so will not only upset the family, but the cemetery's Gatekeeper may bar your way inside the next time you come to the graveyard.

There are also large mausoleums that can be the size of a small public works building, like a school. They can have many floors and wings and may house hundreds of caskets. This is essentially a necropolis, or a city of the dead. If you take the time to search through these structures, you may find many old sections that have been long forgotten. I will often see spirits roaming the hallways visiting other people. It is quite a strange locale, but a wonderful place to do spirit work. These large mausoleums have a different energy than the private family ones. The larger ones feel like a city or great temple. It is easy to imagine that the great halls of the Underworld gods and goddesses must feel quite similar to this.

Tombs and Mounds

Ancient peoples honored the land in such a way that it was very much alive to them. The land is what gave them their food, homes, and everything necessary for survival. The Earth was sacred to them, and it was held in the highest holiness. To people who honored the land as sacred, such as the Celts, the land and the king were one. What happened to one would happen to the other. The king, other royalty, and heroes would be placed in a sacred tomb or burial mound. These became very sacred places over time. They were not places to be frightened of, but places of holiness and spirit.

If we remember, to those people who honored the land in this way, the spirits of the dead were near to and became part of the land. It was common practice to go to the mounds or tombs to seek guidance and wisdom from the spirit of the person buried there. Necromancers would go to these places to seek out the wisdom of the dead spirit's particular profession. If the current king wanted advice about the land or a better way to rule the kingdom, he might go to the mound and petition spirits of former kings for guidance. This was done by sleeping on the mound or in the tomb or by bringing a priest or magician to summon the spirit. By sleeping on a mound, you allowed the spirit who rested within to enter your dreams. Dreams are a gateway into the world of the dead and one of the easiest ways to commune with spirits.

The spirits of kings and warriors had the ability to join with the land after death and become a spirit guardian. The function of a spirit guardian was to protect the land from invaders, aid as oracles, and keep the energies of the land healthy for vegetation. When builders try to tear down some forests and sacred lands, they have sometimes found that their machines have broken down without any explanation. At other times, if a building is built it will have many weaknesses in the structure and may collapse. This is the guardian of that land trying to keep intruders out of the sacred place. There is the tale of the British war chief Vortigern who tried to build a castle, but the castle would not stand and kept tumbling down. Time and time again, Vortigern tried to build the castle and time and time again the castle collapsed. Merlin was called in to do magick to keep the castle standing. When Merlin took a closer look at the land, he found that two dragons, one red and one white, were fighting beneath the Earth and would not allow any structure to stand in that location. When working magically with the land, or simply wanting to build something, it is always best to get the permission of the guardian spirit. Otherwise, you may face many challenges with your endeavor.

It was common to leave offerings in graveyards or the sacred lands of the dead. The bones and remains of the dead were thought to be a powerful link to the Ancestors. The belief was that if one had human bones, one had power over that person. Offerings to the dead included food, wine, honey, blood (both human and animal), material gifts (especially jewelry and other valuables), and flowers.

Graveyard Meditation

One of the best and easiest ways to learn to work with the dead is to contact them at their graves. There are many stories and legends about people going to the cemeteries and grave mounds of kings, heroes, witches, and poets to learn a certain skill or simply to gain advice from that person. Necromancers would also go to graves to summon a spirit to the physical plane, sometimes forcibly. Our purpose here is not to learn how to force a spirit to do something against its will, but rather to learn how to communicate with the spirits of the dead in a very direct way.

If you can find the grave of a teacher within your own profession or the grave of a trusted magician, that would be ideal. Most of the time, however, I ask my Ancestors to guide me to the grave of a spirit that would benefit both of us for this type of work. Sometimes I may see one of my Ancestors walking towards a grave. Other times, I may be "pulled" or "guided" to a grave. Make sure to bring an offering. The most common offerings I use are:

1. Juice
2. Food (bread, cookies, fruit, honey, milk)
3. Coins (silver dollars work well. I usually leave at least two or three)
4. Flowers
5. Water

It is not a good idea to give spirits you are not familiar with alcohol. Alcohol may be too intoxicating for the spirit, and you basically are being introduced to a new spirit who's drunk. Also, we need to keep in mind the spirit's ethics have not changed much since they were alive. If they had a religious taboo against alcohol, then you may be violating their religious beliefs and the spirit may find it disrespectful.

In Greco-Roman necromancy, it is common for magicians to use blood and meat to give the spirit enough energy to manifest and speak with the living. For our purposes here we are giving a token of goodwill and will be visiting the spirit in the astral world and do not need for them to manifest physically. For this meditation, you may go to the graveyard during the day, but if you have access to a graveyard at night, then all the better.

1. Ask your Ancestors to guide you to a grave of someone from

whom both of you can benefit. If you have not found your Ancestors yet, then use your intuition and ask your healing helpers and guides to guide you.

2. Once you have found a grave, take a moment to sense the area. How does it feel? Is it comforting and welcoming? Does it feel as if there is an important task at hand? Does it feel dangerous?

    NOTE: If it feels dangerous and yet your Ancestors and guides want you to work with this spirit, there could be an important reason. If you are beginner, find another grave and come back to it after you have spoken to your Ancestors and guides at some length about what is happening. If you are experienced in necromancy and spirit work, then do the meditation and see what you can do – it may be that the Ancestors wish you to help the spirit for some reason. Do, however, make sure that said reason is congruent with your own ethics.

3. Look at the gravestone and find the name, birth, and death dates of the person. Begin to focus on them. The name of the person acts as an astral beacon and you will be able to call upon the person with just their name.

4. Leave your offering on or near the grave. Try to be as respectful to the grounds as possible. Cemetery keepers do not like it if they perceive that you are leaving "junk" on someone's grave. One of the advantages of liquid, such as milk, honey, or water, is that it is absorbed by the Earth and does not leave anything behind.

5. Sit comfortably on the grave in a meditation posture. Close your eyes and focus on your breathing. Clear your mind of your daily routine and focus on the work at hand.

6. Call out to the spirit of the grave. Ask the spirit if they are willing to meet with you.

7. Begin to imagine yourself seeing the spirit of the grave come to you. How do they look? What clothes are they wearing? Do they look like what you thought they would, or are they different from what you expected?

8. At this point, introduce yourself and ask them questions. You may ask them about their life and what it is like in the afterlife. You may ask them about their profession in life. You may also ask them why your Ancestors chose them. Is there a message the spirit has for you?

9. The spirit may tell you some fascinating things or they may tell you things that are quite ordinary. If they ask you for your help in any way, decide if you are able and willing to aid them in their request. If you can, then great. If not, be polite and explain to them why you cannot help them at this time. If you like, and feel it is appropriate, ask the spirit if it would like to speak with you again. At the end of the conversation, thank the spirit for their time and open your eyes.

10. When you get back home again, make sure you eat, drink, and do things that bring you out of trance and will help you ground.

The Hidden Company

The Hidden Company is a term we use in Traditional Witchcraft. Traditional Witchcraft is Witchcraft that predates modern Wicca and Neo-Paganism. It is said to come from a magical tradition that stretches back to at least the 17th Century and perhaps longer. This kind of magick was more community-based. The witches included in this grouping were the

Wise Women and Cunning Men, Toad Men, Hedge Crafters, and some Shapeshifters. These people practiced in secret to not alert the local authorities of the local town or village. Contrary to the documentation of that era, the townspeople did not always fear these men and women. Western medicine was a far cry from what is today. With little knowledge of surgery and medicine, people often died while in a doctor's care. The townspeople were sometimes poor and could not afford a doctor. The local Hedge Witch or Cunning Man was wise in herb craft, potions, ointments, and magick. At the time they did not call themselves witches. In fact, most of these wise ones were Christian and felt that they were doing the Lord's work by performing healings and magick for the village. To call them a witch was considered an insult, which could bring up charges of heresy against them.

Along with healing, the Traditional Witch also worked with the dead. They had no fear of the dead and often sought out their counsel on a wide variety of subjects. A lot of the old Pagan beliefs were still held by the villagers. There were many rituals for good crops and blessings that would keep good spirits close and malicious spirits far away. To Traditional Witches, the Ancestors were still a part of the greater community. They believed that upon death, the Ancestors stayed with the land.

The Hidden Company were those Ancestors who were witches, healers, and magical people. If you belonged to a group or coven then you had a spiritual lineage to these magical Ancestors. Also, if your family Ancestors were magical then you had lineage through bloodlines. If a witch needed assistance, then they could summon the Hidden Company in ritual. The spirits of witches long gone would come to the ritual space and commune with the living. The Hidden Company were powerful and wise and could help the summoners with spiritual knowledge, wisdom, and magick. They could also aid them in prophecy. One only conjured the Hidden Company when one truly needed their counsel. Today, the Hidden Company are still conjured by Traditional Witches. The Hidden Company are powerful allies to have.

If you belong to an older magical order or coven, then you may conjure the Hidden Company of your group. When treated with the utmost respect, they can help you with your spiritual journey and magick. If you do not belong to a magical order or coven or your group is young, then you may ask to speak to the Hidden Company in general. These would be the spirits of witches and magicians who are willing to aide you in magick even though you do not belong to their magical lineage. These spirits have the ability to add potency to your magick. However, they will only give what is needed and only if they deem you worthy of their influence. I personally never conjure the Ancestors with the intention that they must aid in magick. When they do so it is a benefit and never a requirement. When they lend their powers to you it is a blessing indeed.

The Rose Castle

The Rose Castle is a magical sanctuary for the dead that lies somewhere between the physical plane and the Underworld. It is a place to await the Goddess of Death to take you to the realm of the Ancestors. There is great power and magick in the rose. In magical herb books, the rose is commonly associated with love and sex, but it is much more than that. The rose is an ancient symbol of life, desire, sex, blood, and death. If we allow ourselves to look into the mystery of the rose, we will discover its deeper meanings. Red is the color of birth, life, death, and rebirth. We are born from our mothers covered in blood. This is not something to be disgusted by it is natural and part of the birthing process. The blood that courses through our veins gives us life. Red is also the color of desire and of lust. It is sex that allows the rebirthing process of the future souls to be reborn. Red is also the color of the blood that leaves us at death. Without the magick of blood we die and begin our journey to the Rose Castle.

The Rose Castle was created from desire itself. The realms of the Underworld are created from our dreams and beliefs. The resting place of the Ancestors appears as it does because those who exist there wish it to be so. That is why for the Greco-Romans it appears as Elysium, to the Norse it is Valhalla for warriors and Hel for those not slain in battle, and to the Welsh it is Annwn. For those who follow the path of Traditional Witchcraft there is the Rose Castle. The Rose Castle is a four-walled castle that can be seen when the sun sets over the western seas. During the in-between time of twilight, when the fire of the sun meets the waters of the sea the Rose Castle can be seen.

When the Traditional Witch dies, their spirit is taken to the Rose Castle by a boat or ferryman similar to Charon. Once there, the deceased sees a deserted island with no life. It is barren. There is nothing but the castle itself. This is to keep those away who do not belong here, or perhaps to a spirit whose final resting place is beyond the Island of the Rose Castle. Before the deceased enters the castle, they must have the desire to be with the Goddess. It is desire that created the magick of the castle and it is desire to be with the Goddess of Death that awakens its magick. It is then that the island comes to life, blooming with roses of the afterlife that surround the castle.

The castle is the resting place of the deceased Traditional Witch. It is a place of magick and mystery. The Hidden Company of the witches may be found there. Above all it is the residence of the beautiful and mysterious Goddess of Death. In Traditional Craft she is known as Hulda, Diana, Hecate, Innana, and many other names. She is beautiful and terrible.

She is the magick at the end of desire and the Mother of the Dead who takes us to our place beyond the waves.

Ritual of the Rose Castle

This ritual can be used to meditate upon the Rose Castle and learn about the mysteries, the Goddess of Death, and the Hidden Company. It can also be used to summon the spirits or the goddess to your physical temple.

Items needed

1. A skull. This can be crafted from clay, wood, or ceramic if you do not possess a human skull.
2. 3, 6, or 9 roses
3. Red String, yarn, or chord
4. Four white candles

Place the skull in the center of your working space. This can be used to symbolize the Goddess of Death. Place the roses around the skull. Next, place the four white candles around the skull and roses. Place one in the north first, then south, then east, then west.

Place the red string around the skull and candles making a spiral that is three circuits around counterclockwise. Make sure the space in between is large enough to walk around. The red string is the chord of Fate and it is also the connection of the of your blood to the spirit of the ancestors. It is your direct connection to the dead.

1 Proclaim your intention to the spirits to cross the veils into the Rose Castle to learn about the Hidden Company and the Goddess of Death.
2. Take a moment to center yourself and still your mind. Know that

this is a holy solemn ritual with the intent of a deep understanding or gnosis.

3. Begin at the outer most edge of the spiral of blood/Fate. Begin to walk counterclockwise. At the first circuit, take a moment and contemplate your own death. Your astral body has left the physical plane and you are now on a journey to meet the ancestors. At the second turn, your astral body releases all those things that kept you tethered to the physical plane (relationships, hopes and fears, desires for the future). At the last turn, your spirit is pure, and you feel the power of the connection of the ancestors. The power of the blood and spirit.

4. As you reach the skull, light the white candles in the following order: north then south, east then west. Gaze upon the skull. Visualize the Rose Castle around you coming to life with the bloom of roses. You are in the inner sanctum of the Castle. The skull is the vessel of the Goddess of Death. Call upon her energies and ask her to inhabit the skull for the duration of the ritual. You may visualize the goddess' energies entering the skull.

5. Allow yourself to go into meditation. It is in your mind and heart that the Ancestors will come to visit you. What do you see? Close your eyes and see if the Ancestors come to you in vision. Visualize the Goddess of Death manifesting in the skull. You may spend some time speaking with her. What wisdom does she give you? If you like, you can also summon the Ancestors and the Goddess of Death to the physical plane. This takes more magical power and can be done alone or in a group.

6. When you are finished, thank the Ancestors and the Goddess of Death. Visualize the ancestors and the Goddess returning to the

Underworld. Extinguish the candles.

7. Begin your journey back to the world of the living. Begin your journey by walking clockwise. At the first turn, you re-affirm that the ancestors are always around you acting as guides. At the second turn, you remember who you are (your desires, your hopes and fears, your dreams for the future). At the third turn, you enter your physical body and return to the physical plane.

This is a powerful and profound ritual and is one of my favorites. To me, there is nothing like being with the Goddess of Death and the Hidden Company in this manner. It seems like a simple ritual, but it holds much power and gnosis. Please remember to center and ground after this working and journal your experience.

Summoning Spirits of the Dead

To call upon the spirits of the dead in magick and ritual is a practice as old as magick itself. Every pagan culture from the Greeks to the Egyptians had rituals to call upon the dead. It was not seen as evil or diabolic until the patriarchal religions came into power. This is because Christian cultures taught that the dead were either in heaven or hell never to return and you were not summoning the dead, you were summoning demons. Pagans did not share this philosophy. To summon the spirits of the dead was as common as it was to summon deities in ritual. When we summon the dead in magick it can be for many reasons such has healing, wisdom, finding lost objects, and oracle work, to name a few purposes. I have given you a basic ritual outline below. This is a simple outline that is taught to magicians. It is only a suggested outline. If you would like to come up with something different that works better for you, by all means please do. This is just to get you started using a traditional formula.

Ritual Outline

I.   Purpose for summoning the dead

Before doing any magick, no matter what it is, you must have a purpose. You must decide what it is you want from the spirit and whether or not it is worth their time. Put yourself in their shoes. You would not want someone pulling you out of a perfectly happy afterlife just because they wanted to see if they could do it. You may do a divination such as with runes or tarot to see if it is a favorable time for this type of magick.

II.   Establishing sacred space

It is important that we have a safe and comfortable space for the spirits when we call to them. You do not want any distractions or energies that may take away from the experience.

Cleansing/banishing

The first thing you will need to do is cleanse and banish the space. If you are working indoors you will need to physically clean your ritual space. You will also need to cleanse the space magically to get rid of any negative energies that may inhibit your work. Also, as a rule of thumb, negative energies attract negative spirits. We want to be as spiritually clean as possible. For banishing, you may simply use a witch's broom to sweep away the negative energies or if you prefer a more ceremonial technique you can perform the Kabbalistic Lesser Banishing Ritual of the Pentagram. You may find this ritual in Donald Michael Kraig's book *Modern Magick: Twelve Lessons in the High Magickal Arts*.

You may use the Lesser Banishing Ritual of the Pentagram or you may use a modified version of the ritual below to banish unwanted energies.

The Pentagram Rite of Protection

1. Stand in the middle of your temple area facing East. Say a prayer to the gods that you fallow. If you have not chosen a god or goddess, you can pray to the creator or the Universe. Ask the gods to protect you and your temple space.

2. Walk to the eastern part of your temple room. With your dominate hand trace a flaming blue pentagram in the air, beginning at the bottom left point, draw clockwise. Know that it will protect your temple space from negative energies and banish unwanted energies as well.

3. Place both hands over the center of the pentagram and call to your god or goddess and say, "I call upon the highest power of (name of god/Universe). May this pentagram protect all those who stand within."

4. Go to the southern part of your temple room. With your dominate hand trace a flaming blue pentagram in the air, beginning at the bottom left point. Place both hand over the center and say, "I call upon the highest spirit of (name of god/Universe). May this pentagram protect all those who stand within."

5. Go to the western part of your temple room. With your dominate hand trace a flaming blue pentagram in the air, beginning at the bottom left point. Place both hand over the center and say, "I call upon the highest being of (name of god/Universe). May this pentagram protect all those who stand within."

6. Go to the northern part of your temple room. With your dominate hand trace a flaming blue pentagram in the air, beginning at the bottom left point. Place both hand over the center and say, "I

call upon the highest form of (name of god/Universe). May this pentagram protect all those who stand within."

7. Return to the center of the temple space. Visualize all four pentagrams surrounding your temple with bright light. Know that all those you conjure may enter your temple. All others cannot.

Circle

When working with the dead, I personally do not draw a circle because I treat the dead exactly how I would treat a visitor in my home. I would never say, "Excuse me Sir, please stand beyond this boundary because I do not know you." I also understand that as a beginner you may feel the need for a magical circle to keep out unfamiliar spirits. At this time draw your circle, if you are going to do so, using your tool of choice such as an athame, dagger, broom, or your index finger. Just remember to visualize your circle as a sphere or dome of flaming blue light.

Stand in the east with your athame, broom, or dagger. Visualize your tool absorbing powerful spiritual energy from the Universe. See your tool glowing with power. Project the energy out from your tool and create a powerful blue arc from above your head down into the floor. Half of the arc is in your temple the other half is under the floor. You will create a solid sphere. Place your tool to the side of the arc and visualize your tool sending out energy as you open the arc to form a perfect sphere. Take your time as you open the arc and walk to the south, then west, then north. Finally, join the arc in the east forming your sphere of light. Stand in the center of your protective sphere and feel the power of the sphere.

Calling Gods, Ancestors, Nature Spirits

You will want to call upon the gods that you work with to oversee the ritual. However you prefer to call them is fine. If you do not have a specific god and goddess that you work with, simply ask that the Great God and Goddess who created all things be present and watch over your ritual. I also call the Ancestors that I work with to be present. Make sure that you invite your Ancestors into your circle. They are honored guests and should be treated as such. The circle will allow them in. A magick circle only keeps out the things you want out. Otherwise, the gods and other spirits are welcome in. If you work with nature spirits, elves, faeries, and the like, feel free to welcome them into your space if you know them well and trust them.

III. Vessel or catalyst

In the beginning of your necromantic work, you may find it helpful to use something that the spirits of the dead can use to reside and manifest in while they are in your magical space. It takes a lot of energy for the dead to manifest in the physical and/or astral plane, so having a place for them to reside will help them tremendously. When you become an advanced practitioner, you will not need a catalyst because you can simply use magical energy for them to manifest. However, do not do this until you are adept at summoning spirits.

Incense smoke

One suggestion for a catalyst is a fumigation. There are many herbs that resonate with the energies of the dead. A few of them are mugwort, wormwood, dittany of Crete, myrrh, dragon's blood, bay leaf, and flax seed. Simply purchase or make a blend you prefer and burn on non-toxic charcoal briquettes. A couple of recommendation for books on this are *The Complete Book of Incense, Oils, and Brews* by Scott Cunningham and *The*

Element Encyclopedia of 5000 Spells by Judika Illes. Remember, toxins drain the spirit's energy. Burning non-toxic charcoal will help the spirit manifest easier. When the spirit manifests, it is common to see the shape of the person's face in the smoke. It sounds funny but remember to crack a window or you may have the smoke alarm going off in the middle of your ritual, which is very disruptive.

Poppet

Again, it takes a large amount of energy for the dead to manifest in the physical plane. You may use a poppet to can act as a "house" for the spirit to temporarily reside in. The figure can be cloth or wax. It is traditional to use beeswax, but paraffin works well too. When you do your conjurations, tell the spirit of the dead that it may use the poppet as a vessel for the duration of the ritual. Some magicians believe that you use one doll per spirit and never use one doll for many different spirits. This is because the spirit leaves an energetic signature, and it confuses the new spirit. If you choose not to work with a spirit ever again, make sure you gently release the spirit from the poppet, send it back to where it came from, burn the doll, and then bury it as if it were a corpse. This will sever the tie between you and the spirit.

Skull and Bones

The skull and bones is one of the most ancient and primal forms of necromancy. The bones have an energy signature close to that of the energy of when the spirit was alive. There is also a connection with re-animation, but you will not re-animate the spirit with the bones, only communicate with it. This is one of the strongest vessels you can use. You may use just a skull or other parts of the skeleton. Traditionalists say to always use real human bones and never replicas. I say that the mind of the magician is the power behind all magick and if a skull replica works for you then by all means use it. Using a skull replica for housing the spirit will also give your ritual a "necromantic" feeling and often adds more energy to the ceremony simply because it touches a deep part of our mind that honors death.

Candles

Most of the time the ancients did not use candles in their necromantic rites. If there was fire, it was a small bonfire or the flames from an oil lamp. Personally, being in the modern age, I will sometimes use black or white candles to give the spirit more energy to manifest. Black candles traditionally symbolize the night, dark magick, the Underworld, the dead, and the Great Mystery. White candles symbolize purity, the divine, pure spirit, day, cleansing. I leave it up to your intuition to use what is right for you.

If you want to be inspired by the Greco-Romans, you may use a cauldron fire to give the spirits energy in your rite. Pour a little rubbing alcohol in an iron or metal bowl or cauldron and light it with a match. Remember a little goes a long way.

IV. Offerings

It is proper to give the spirits you are working with offerings; be it gods, nature spirits or the Ancestors. Offerings give the spirits more energy to manifest. It is also a good gesture of energy exchange. If they do something for you, you do something for them. It is important to remember to only give offerings to spirits that are helpful. Never give offerings to demons or destructive or trickster spirits. They may take your good gesture and do negative or harmful deeds with it.

Milk, water, incense, wine, honey, blood, beans, flax

These are traditional offerings to the dead. Offerings that have large amounts of life force give the spirits a large amount of energy. I do not recommend that beginners use blood as an offering, because this will give a spirit so much energy that it may be hard to get rid of them. Think of it as if you are giving someone heroin. It will give them a powerful high, but the spirits (like people) may sometimes do anything to get it again, even turning vampiric. This is very troublesome. Wine is a good substitute for blood.

Flowers and gifts

Sometimes flowers and gifts such as toys, trinkets, and knick-knacks are given to show appreciation. Each region and religion have different things that they give. My personal favorite is when some Asian cultures give the dead fireworks and spirit money. They burn the money so the dead have plenty of money in the Afterlife.

V. The Conjuration of Manifestation

When you call upon the spirits of the dead, there are a variety of ways you may do this. If you prefer the ancient ways of the Egyptians, Greeks, Romans, or Babylonians, there is a very definite structure. The Greeks would ask the Gatekeeper Hecate to open the doors to the Underworld. Then they petitioned Persephone the Queen of the Underworld, with the name of the spirit they wished to summon.

It would look something like this:

> "Great goddess Hecate! Lady of the crossroads and the keeper of the Keys, I ask that you open the gates to Hades. Blessed be your powers to protect us from harmful spirits and to prepare us for the journey ahead.
>
> "Beautiful Goddess Persephone, Queen of Hades, Mother of the Dead! I ask that you find it in your gracious heart to allow the shade of (person's full name) to journey the death road back to the

realm of the living for a short time so that I may (purpose of ritual).

"I ask that (person's full name) journey forth into the world of the living for the purpose of (purpose of ritual). I ask that they remain here for the duration of this ritual until you are dismissed by me and the power of the gods summoned here tonight."

It is important to know that the Romans seldom conjured the name of Hades. Hades was the Lord of the Dead and to conjure him or to speak his name was to bring death and chaos into your temple or grove. He was respected, but greatly feared. Persephone on the other hand, was a goddess who dwelt half of the year in the Middleworld with her mother Demeter and could understand the desires and shortcomings of man. She had great love and sympathy for their suffering, and she would help them in any way she could. When this conjuration was used, it was common to give Hecate and Persephone offerings of love and gratitude.

If you follow other pantheons, you may substitute other names. Remember to call upon the god or goddess that opens the gates to the Underworld and then the god or goddess of the Underworld itself. If you do not know the Gatekeeper, you may simply say the conjuration of the God/dess and the shade desired. Remember that the above conjuration is something I modified from ancient Greco-Roman necromancy. If you would like to come up with your own summoning, you are certainly welcome. You can even be a little simpler and say something like this:

"I call to the gatekeeper who opens the gates between this world and the world of the dead. Open for me the gates to the Underworld. God and Goddess of the dead, we ask that you allow

(Name of Spirit) to travel from the world beyond to the physical world of here and now."

VI. Communications

This is the "meat" of the ritual, or the point where the purpose of the ritual comes to fruition. Everything up to this point prepared you, your space, and the spirits for this moment. This is a very sacred act. In medieval grimoires of necromancy, a spirit of the dead was sometimes threatened and commanded like a servant. One reason for this was because it was thought that necromancy was unholy and diabolical, and the spirits were really devils anyway and should be treated as such. Another reason was because of the fear of death and the spirits of the dead. Magicians feared that the spirits could jump into the magick circle and take the magician kicking and screaming down into the depths of hell. This all comes from Christian superstition and fear. In ancient pagan indigenous cultures, the dead were a part of the community and were to be welcomed and blessed. The rituals were simply to help the dead manifest in a way that the living could see and understand in a more profound way. The spirits of the dead are welcomed guests. Treat them as such.

I like to tell my students, "You would never invite someone into your home and start yelling at them: "Hey you!!! Stand in the corner and answer my questions or I'm gonna smack the crap out of you!" Being rude to the dead is the same thing.

I have listed only a few reasons one may wish to summon the dead. There are many others, but remember what we have talked about before. To summon any spirit, you must have a specific purpose. You would not be too happy if someone called your phone and asked you to come to their house and after you got there they said, "I only asked you to come over just to see if you would. Goodbye now!"

Divination

The spirits of the dead can see how events flow through the Underworld before they manifest in the Middleworld. They are not bound by time and space, and they can also travel back and forth in time and witness events firsthand. This is why the ancients used the dead in divination. We are reminded of how Odin conjured the seeress in the Underworld to know the fate of his son, Baldur. We must remember that the dead have hopes, fears, and prejudices just as we do, and they are not always removed from the situation you may be asking about. They also may interpret information their own way. We all know that three people can witness a car accident and then all offer different interpretations when questioned. Personally, I only use my Ancestors and specific spirits for divination, however I encourage you to experiment and come up with your own conclusions.

Teachings about Death, Vocation, Underworld, and Wisdom

The dead can be valuable when they are questioned about death and the Underworld. They have firsthand experience when it comes to what it was like to transition into the Afterlife and what their experiences are in the Underworld. This may help prepare us for the death process. It also can give people peace of mind from their own anxieties about death and whether there actually is an Afterlife. It is helpful to know that your beloved family member is happy where they are after death. Also, it was common for ancient cultures to ask the dead about their vocation. There are many stories of artists and poets sleeping on the burial mound of a great artist hoping to meet them in dreams to ask their advice. You may also conjure the spirit of a magician or witch to ask them information about magick. I will warn you though, not every spirit wishes to be conjured to the physical plane. I would ask my Ancestors to find them and ask them personally if they would not mind coming to you during your ritual.

Closure

It may be important for you to conjure the dead for yourself or on behalf of someone who may need closure. If things were left unsaid or perhaps there was a great quarrel that left deep energetic wounds in the family, the spirit may be conjured to give closure for both parties. This is wonderful healing if it is done with love. When a ritual to call the dead is done for this purpose the spirit may still be angry and they may need to hear an apology or vice versa. Sometimes when there is an accident or death comes very suddenly, we do not have the time we would like to say our goodbyes. This is the time to do it. This can be very therapeutic. It allows both parties to move on and sever energetic chords that may be keeping them stuck in grief and frustration.

Unquiet Spirit

Hauntings do not happen very often, but they do indeed happen. If someone is experiencing unexplained phenomena such as items going missing, cabinets and drawers slamming, a chill in the room when the window is closed, or a "presence," you may have a haunting. There can be several reasons that a place is haunted, and you may need to conjure the dead to find out what to do to pacify the spirit. They may have unfinished business, or they may not know they are dead. They may be seeking justice for something. There are many other possible reasons. Conjuring the dead and finding out what to do is the best way to rid yourself of a haunting.

VII. Dismissing the spirit of the dead

After you are finished speaking with the spirit you will need to dismiss them. You may simply thank them and give them a blessing on their way back to the Underworld or you may use a more formal speech such as:

> "(Name of spirit) I thank you for your attendance here tonight. I ask that you return to the Afterlife (or Hades, Hel, etc.) harming none on your way.

> "Goddess Persephone, take your child back into your arms where they are forever safe.

> "Mighty Hecate, I ask that you light the way for (name of spirit) and close the gates of Hades. I thank you mighty Queen!"

VIII. Thanking the Dead and Gods, Ancestors, and spirits

After your conjuration is concluded you must thank the spirits, Ancestors, nature spirits, and gods for coming to your ritual space. I personally do not banish them in the traditional sense, but I will thank them for their energies and help, and welcome them to stay in my space if they like (but only if they are known and trusted spirits). If you cast a circle, dismantle it at this point. Leave appropriate offerings to the gods and spirits as you see fit.

IX. Banishing space

If, after your conjurations, you feel negative energy in your ritual space or feel like you may attract unwanted entities with your workings, then banish them from your space. Use the same procedure you used in the beginning to cleans and banish.

The Dead and Cursing

There are many old grimoires that speak of conjuring the dead to curse an enemy. This makes sense because in medieval grimoires, it was thought that the spirit of our Ancestors went to Heaven or Hell and they would not be able to help us in magick. It was only the tormented Earthbound spirits who were able to cause sickness, pain, and misfortune for one's intended target. These spirits were only too happy to cause harm to another because they knew nothing but torment and misery. In my personal work with the Ancestors and other spirits of the dead, my magick is used for healing, education, and wisdom. It is never meant to command the dead to do my bidding, especially to harm someone. It is important to know that it is possible to hurt another person, and there are some unethical magicians who have no problem at all with causing pain and suffering to others no matter what the cost. Binding spirits of the dead to harm another is extremely dangerous. If the spirit is ever freed, they may seek revenge on the dark magician (and rightly so). Never think that you are above the power of the Underworld Gods. These gods treat the dead as their children and will harm you if you harm them. I have known a few magicians who have used spirits, the dead, and other entities to harm others. This caused them psychological pain and suffering in the long run. Also, spirits talk to one another. The dead will not want to work with you if you have a reputation for causing harm to people or other spirits.

Healing and Removing Curses

The spirits of the dead can be used to help heal and to remove curses from someone or something. As we have talked about, the Ancestors have a stronger influence in the astral plane and the spirit world. They can see energies more clearly than we can and can aid us in strengthening or weakening those energies. When it comes to healing, they may ask other entities of healing to help us. They may also be able to direct the energies in a more direct way than we are able to see or know. They can also weaken the energies of dark magick that are sent against us. If a spirit is causing the harm, then they can speak with that spirit and try to convince it to not harm us. They can also energetically weaken the magical stream that is being sent to us. For us to do this, we just simply have to ask them for help. I will visualize what I would like the Ancestors to do. They can see what you see and sometimes it is easier to show them than it is to explain it to them.

Forcing the Dead Against Their Will

I would like to take this opportunity to talk about using magick to force or bind the dead to do things that are against their will. In this book, we have discussed how important it is to treat all spirits with respect, be it gods, nature spirits, planetary entities, Ancestors, or spirits of the dead that you do not know. There are some magical practitioners who use magick to bind the dead and force them to do things even if they spirit wants to or not. You can find many books on necromancy, especially in medieval magick, that have pages and pages of cursing spirits of the dead and binding them to work the will of the magician.

Let us take a moment to discuss why magicians from long ago would do such a thing. Were magicians of the past unethical? The answer is not necessarily. In medieval times, magick and witchcraft were outlawed in Europe. Pagans and healers who worked with the Ancestors would not have written their magick down, and if they did, it would have not been available for anyone to see. Some ceremonial magicians did write down their magical techniques. Ceremonial magicians primarily came from a Judeo-Christian background. In this belief system, any spirit that was not an angel from God was considered a demon from Hell or at best a mischievous spirit that needed to be controlled. Most grimoires talked about how to bind spirits and force them to do the will of the magician. They also most likely believed that if you were a spirit that could be conjured and bound then obviously you were not allowed into Heaven and you were supposed to be in Hell. To their way of thinking, there was nothing wrong with commanding a spirit of the dead that was supposed to be in Hell anyway. You may be horrified at this philosophy, but in that time, this was a common belief of Europeans, and this is all they knew of earthbound spirits.

There are some modern practices that have mixed traditions with ceremonial magick. Sometimes, when this happens, the magician may still believe that spirits of the dead who are earthbound, lost, or conjured from the Underworld (Hell in their point of view) deserve to be bound and controlled. The spiritual philosophy that I have presented here is far from those ideas.

Again, all spirits should be respected. Not all Ancestors or the dead have our best intent in mind. As we have learned, just because you have passed on from the physical plane into the Otherworld does not mean that instantaneously you become wise and evolve. It just means you are dead. The only time the dead should be bound is if they are causing sickness or harm to the living and then they should only be bound long enough for a healing spirit of the Underworld to come and take them to the proper place to be, a place of learning and healing, not a place of torment and damnation. When using the magical techniques of necromancy and Ancestor work, you must treat all spirits with the utmost respect, compassion, and honor. If you are careless, indignant, or cruel to the dead, then eventually the dead may turn on you. Remember, as you get older and weaker your magick may waver. The dead that you have upset have literally all the time in the world. The dead can be very patient when they want to be.

When you treat spirits as family, friends, and colleagues, they will treat you with love and respect. I would much rather a spirit help me out of love and friendship than to have to force them to do anything. When you have a relationship with the dead out of mutual respect, the work can be rewarding.

Re-Animation
The Sorrow of Isis (Egyptian)

The great Mother Goddess of Egypt, Isis, had left her son, Horus, in the company of the gods while she was away curing a child who had been stung by a scorpion. The gods took great care of Horus, who would one day become the ruler of the cosmos. As Horus played by himself, scorpions scuttled across the floor. The gods took great care to keep the child-god protected from anyone who wished him harm, but they did not see the little creatures creeping down below. Before anyone knew what had happened, Horus was stung. His body lay motionless on the ground and foam spilled from his mouth. The gods did not know what to do. None of them had the power to return the dead back to life.

As Isis returned home, she was told the terrible news of her son. The Great Mother leaped to her son's side and held him close to her. She saw the wound where the poison had entered his little body. "Horus is stung!" She cried. "Horus is stung!"

Nephthys, with tears in her eyes, went to Isis and said, "Isis, pray to the skies so that the spirits who row the great barge of Ra will stop their rowing. The sun barge will forever sit over the place where Horus lies until Ra restores the little one to life."

In her anguish, Isis let out a cry for her dead child that only a mother could. The cry was directed to those who rowed the barge of Ra. The bright disk above stopped. Not one of them had the heart to continue. The sorrow of Isis was too much for them. They were frozen by her cries. Then, Thoth appeared before Isis and her little son. He saw Isis' tears and felt great pity for her. "Isis do not cry for your son. Ra himself gave me the power of Ma'at! All things I say come to pass. For Ma'at is the law, and thus my word is law."

Isis held Horus tightly as Thoth approached. He held the little one's hands and spoke the magical words over his head that brought Horus back to life. He spoke of the protection the cosmos would provide for the little god in the Middleworld, Underworld, and Upperworld. He spoke of the adventures and triumphs he would have in days to come. He spoke of a boy who would grow up to be a fierce and honorable warrior. He spoke of a divine life. As Thoth spoke, so it came to pass. Horus returned to life and grew up to be an honorable and strong warrior.

Fears of Re-Animation

When it comes to working with the dead and necromancy, re-animation is the most controversial topic there is. In almost every religious philosophy, to re-animate the dead is the biggest taboo. In many stories, to do so has dire, even deadly consequences. I would like to discuss the topic and try to help the reader understand the reasons for re-animation. There are two common reasons to bring the dead back to life. The first would be when a loved one has been killed and the grieving family members and friends wish their loved one to be returned to them. The second is more diabolical. It is when dark necromancers wish to have control over the dead for a variety of reasons. When we examine the reasons for bringing a loved one back to life, it is hard not to be sympathetic to those people who are grieving. Almost everyone has wished that a friend or family member who has been taken away could stand before them in the flesh again. This is especially true when one's child or spouse is murdered or killed by accident. We tell ourselves that they died too young and that if only the situation was different they would still be alive. When magicians and witches are overcome with grief and they understand that they have real power, there may be a thought in the back of their mind that says: "What if?" When someone is grieving, their thoughts and actions may not always be rational. Grief is powerful. Our desire to have our loved one back may be equally as powerful. There are many myths and legends of how the grieving have used magick, or hired someone to use magick, to bring back a loved one. Nowadays, most ethical magicians and witches would not consider such a thing. They would, however, have sympathy for the grieving person and help them through the pain of loss. But in the past, some magicians have not been so ethical. There are many stories of re-animation gone wrong. There are stories of the spirit of the dead being forced back into a rotting corpse and feeling the bewilderment and pain of being in a broken body.

There are myths of mortals, and even gods, seeking the aid of Underworld Gods to bring their loved one back to life. The gods of the dead almost always decline the request. However, once in a great while, they may grant the wish. But bringing the dead back to life always has special requirements. There is always some sort of magical "catch" and usually the mortal, and even the gods, fail at the requirements needed to bring back the dead. My personal belief is that when a strong mortal or god makes such a request to the Dark Gods, the gods understand that sometimes there is no reasoning with one who is grieving so the requirements they place upon resurrection are intentionally very tricky. I believe they know that the supplicant will fail and the dead will safely remain with the Ancestors. But what of the gods who have succeeded, such as Osiris, and Jesus, and the like? If we take the myth of the resurrected god as a story, then it was written in a period of agricultural reliance and the people needed myths to explain the seasons of the sun and the cycles of the crops. Even though the crops died in the winter, they would be resurrected in the spring. If we take the resurrected gods as more than myth, then upon further inspection, we discover that the gods that died and returned to life have a shamanic initiation. What happens during a shamanic initiation is that the god or hero seeks to understand the mysteries of death and dies, at least temporarily. We see this in such myths as the Death of Osiris and the Descent of Inanna; also, with the sacrifice of Odin on the World Tree. When a god dies, it throws off the cosmic balance. The Universe intervenes in some way to restore the balance, otherwise the worlds will be thrown into chaos and death and destruction will rule in the place of life and order. The Universe may intervene in several different ways. One such way is that another god or gods seek to bring back the deceased gods through resurrection. When Set killed his brother Osiris, Isis searched the world for his body parts in order to bring him back to life to restore cosmic balance. While Inanna's sister imprisoned her in the Underworld, the Earth's vegetation and crops died. To stop this from happening, other spirits and gods conspired to help Inanna escape and return to the celestial realms. However, after the resurrection of the gods from the Underworld, they return with the understanding of the mystery of life and death.

There are stories about dark magicians, necromancers, and witches who used magick to bring the dead back to life for their own diabolical purposes. You can find many "old" grimoires that describe in detail how to bring back the spirit of the dead in order to re-animate a corpse. There were several different reasons that one might want to bring the dead back to life as a necromancer. One reason is to temporally re-animate the corpse for divination and prophecy. Once the spirit was summoned into his or her corpse, they compelled them with magick to answer their questions. This took great skill and powerful magick. The magician or witch had to find a certain spirit in the Underworld with incantations and spells, and then force them to return to their corpse, and then bind them to the corpse for a certain amount of time. On top of that, they must compel them to tell the truth of future events. The whole process was considered painful for the spirit and was considered unethical even in ancient times.

The necromancer did not have to summon a spirit into the corpse that they once inhabited in life. The spirit could be summoned into any corpse the magician chose. This was even worse for the spirit. The corpse could be in any shape of deterioration and because it did not belong to the spirit of the dead in life it was harder to inhabit. Yet with great magick, the necromancer could bind the spirit to the corpse to speak prophecies.

A witch or magician could also use a severed head or simply a skull that was consecrated to the work of necromancy. The magical process was similar to that of binding the spirit to a corpse, but in this instance, it was bound temporarily to the skull. The magician only needed to hear the utterings of prophecies, so it did not need the whole body. It only needed the skull to speak. The skull would have magical sigils and incantations written on the crown, the jaw, and inside the cranium. There are also spells that require magicians to put magical writings on bay leaves and insert them in the skull's mouth. The necromancer then summoned the spirit of the dead into the skull for the spirit to mutter prophecies. The prophecies that the magician often sought out were mostly political in nature. It was most desirable to know the inner workings of the courts and minds of emperors and kings of the ancient world. Very often, someone would seek out a necromancer to hear the dark prophecies of a skull or talking head. This was usually an enemy of the state or someone from the opposing country looking to find the weakness of the rulers to defeat them in battle.

Asclepius and Diana Bring Back the Dead (Greco-Roman)

Hippolytus was the son of Theseus. He was a vibrant youth who had strength and a great deal of wisdom at an early age. His stepmother, Phaedra, was close to him in age and fell in love with him. She tried to seduce him, but Hippolytus would not betray his father in such a dishonorable way. Phaedra was furious! No one dared to reject the beauty of the princess, for she was daughter of King Minos of Crete. She would have revenge on him! She was a devotee of the god Poseidon and prayed to him to seek revenge upon the boy.

One day, Hippolytus was driving his chariot close to the seashore, when a giant sea monster rose from the depths. The hideous creature splashed with a mighty roar and the horses driving the chariot were frightened. They ran away from the creature dragging the chariot with them. The monster chased after the chariot and with one mighty swing, the chariot was smashed to bits. Asclepius, the god of healing, found Hippolytus. The poor boy was dead. There was no longer breath in his beautiful young body. Asclepius wept for this tragedy.

The Goddess Diana of the Moon heard her nephew weeping. She descended from the heavens and appeared before Asclepius.

"Lady," Asclepius wept, "the poor boy is dead and my magick alone cannot bring him back to life."

Diana felt Asclepius' heartache and decided to help him. "Each of our powers alone cannot bring the poor boy back. But you have the power to heal, and I have the power of mystery. Together, we may bring the boy to life."

Asclepius reached deep within himself and called upon the powers of healing that he received from his father, Apollo, and was instructed in by the centaur, Charon. His magick swelled up inside him until he could no longer restrain it. He touched the wounds of Hippolytus and sent forth the power of healing. Diana added her magick of mystery and the two gods' powers intertwined like a spiral of two serpents writhing around each other. For a moment, the Earth did not move, the bees did not harvest nectar, and the sun did not journey across the sky. Suddenly, Hippolytus opened his eyes. His death wounds were healed. Diana then took the boy away from his cruel stepmother and sent him to be protected by a nymph named Egeria.

My Thoughts on Modern Re-animation

Bringing back someone from the dead is something that almost every culture forbids or at least gives dire warnings against. Several cultures speak of it as being only a temporary fix that goes against the ebb and flow of nature. In some ancient cultures, it was a crime against the state and in others it was a crime against the gods. Most magical people either could not, or would not, bring the dead back to life. However, that does not mean that it was not done. There are spells and rituals that necromancers would use to temporarily summon the spirit of the dead into a rotting corpse. This ghoulish magick was intended to bring the necromancer information from the Underworld bringing knowledge that most magicians would never have.

I personally believe that there are far more productive ways to work with spirits of the dead than re-animating a corpse. The more you work with the dead the easier it will become to see them, feel their presence, and to speak with them. I believe that the ancient spells used to re-animate a corpse were used because those magicians did not have the psychic skill to see nor hear the dead without the aid of a body. They also did not possess the skill to channel the spirit within their own body. Part of that was because they feared possession by spirits of the dead. The truth is, it is harder than you think for a spirit of the dead to possess and take control of your body. However, the ancient necromancers did not want to take that chance.

Say, for instance, that you had the power and skill to bring back a person who had just died or recently died. The person originally died because the body was damaged in some way that the body could not support life. The circumstances behind the death could be anything including old age, trauma, or disease. The body could not sustain life on its own. To have a minimal chance for success, you needed a master necromancer and a master healer as in the case of Asclepius and Diana. Even then, it took the two gods to bring one person back to life. When the person revived, Asclepius was punished by the King of the Gods himself.

I believe that when we obtain the gifts and blessings of the spirits and gods, we need to respect them and the natural flow of the Universe. To go against these principles would have bad karmic consequences for everyone involved. I continue to believe that there is a reason for everything. Sometimes the reason for a loved one's untimely death is beyond the understanding of mortals and the Ancestors. If we go against that flow of energy, then we can throw things out of balance. The spirits can and will intervene. You also risk losing the gifts that the spirits gave you.

As we advance in our magick evolution we will gain insight and power. Some of that power we will learn through working with the dead.

The dead can be powerful allies and guardians. They can help us turn back curses aimed at us and even aid us in healing. The dead can teach us their skills from beyond the grave. However, the dead should be treated with the utmost respect. The dead are not devils or spirits who will give us disease or bring death upon us, they are spirits who should be honored. When we work with the dead with honor, they will become powerful teachers who show us the mysteries of death, the Underworld, and when we are trusted they may show us deeper into the Great Mystery.

5
Skulls, Bones, and Blood

Odin Enchants Mimir's Head (Norse)

All-Father held the head of his dear friend. Poor Mimir was killed because the Gods of the Vanir felt cheated. After the great war between the Aesir and Vanir, two hostages of the Aesir were given to the Vanir: the wise Mimir and the less-wise Hoenir. In exchange, the Vanir gave Njord, Freyr, and Freya as hostages. The Vanir soon realized that without Mimir, Hoenir did not speak wise counsel. The Vanir were outraged. In retaliation, Mimir was returned to Odin without his body. All-Father could not bear to have his friend sent to the Halls of Hel.

Odin had powerful magick. He had the runes, and he had the enchantments of the Nine Worlds. Using the powers of the runes and his spells, Odin returned Mimir's head back to life. He used special resins to keep the head preserved. He put magical herbs inside the head to summon back the spirit of Mimir. Finally, with the runes he brought the head of Mimir to life once more. Mimir opened his eyes to see All-Father staring back at him. Odin took Mimir and placed him deep in the Underworld in a magical well. The well had magical powers of wisdom and life. Mimir would drink from the magick well and utter prophecies and wisdom to those who journeyed into its mysteries.

The Skull

One symbol of witchcraft, magick, and necromancy is the skull. The skull is the symbol of death in all cultures and in all time periods throughout history. By simply gazing upon the human skull our minds can be filled with thoughts of death and the afterlife. In modern times, the human skull serves as a warning to be careful, such as in a warning for danger or poison, or else we, too, may become nothing more than a skull. The skull reminds us that death is imminent. We are born and we must die. No one is safe from death. For a lot of people in our modern world, the skull can be a sorrowful symbol of the grief of having lost a loved one or the grotesque images of a body rotting down deep in the grave.

The skull has been used in magick ever since the first shaman began to understand the physical and spiritual components of death. Let us take a moment to have a further understanding of what the skull is. Physically, the skull is the bone structure that forms our head. It has a protective cranium for our brains, eye sockets, a mandible with our teeth, and nose holes for breathing. Without this structure we could not live.

When ancient tribespeople died, their bodies decomposed and all that remained was their bones. Their bones seemed to be eternal and did not decompose as fast as the rest of the body. Ancient people must have been fascinated by this. They looked at the bones as magical because they had the power to survive even after death. To ancient people this was great magick from the gods themselves! As the only part of the body of their loved ones that remained, surely they must still hold the essence of that person. Perhaps a little part of the deceased was still energetically present.

In an energetic and spiritual sense, the skull and bones were connected to the energies of death—not necessarily to bring death to this world or to a person, but to understand that death was a part of the natural cycle of life. The spiritually minded person understands that the only thing that remains after death is the spirit. So, because the skull and bones were the only things that remained and the spirit was the only energetic thing that remained after death, the only logical conclusion to draw was that the skull was a representation of the human spirit.

When magical people use the skull and bones in their work, they do so for a variety of reasons and there are many ways to do it. One of the most common ways to use the skull in magick was to create a "Talking Head." Talking Heads were primarily found in Celtic lands and parts of Europe. As previously stated, the ancient Celts were headhunters and would keep the head of their enemy as a trophy because they believed that the soul resided there. The human skull would be enchanted to summon a divination spirit and the skull would then utter prophecies of the future. It is speculated that only a skilled necromancer could hear the words of the talking head, but there have been stories told that any passer-by would be able to hear the magical skull speak. After Alexander the Great was killed, his head was placed in a jar of honey. Honey is a natural preservative. It was said that Greek emperors would ask the talking head of Alexander for advice before going to war or before any great act of leadership.

The skull can also be used as a permanent or temporary vessel for spirits in magick. When the magician summons a spirit of the dead, it takes a large amount of energy for the spirit to be able to occupy the physical plane. For spirits to become effective in divination or carrying out tasks, they need energy from us. They need offerings and a temporary vessel. The most gruesome vessel would be the rotting corpse itself. Historically in most cultures, using necromancy to re-animate a corpse or using a decomposing body for spirit work was illegal because it desecrated the honor and memory of the body, and it was a grotesque and time-consuming act. One had to dig up a grave or break into a crypt and then summon the spirit into the rotting body. If I were a spirit, I most certainly would not want to find myself in the body of a corpse with rotting limbs and a foul stench. A more civilized way to create a vessel for a spirit to use in necromancy would be to use a human skull. Once the session was over, the spirit would be released from the skull and the skull would then be physically and spiritually cleansed.

The skull can also be used as a gateway or portal when journeying into the Underworld. Each eye socket, nostril, ear hole, and the mouth are a gateway into a different part of the Underworld and the Realm of the Dead. The important thing to remember about such portals is that they may or may not always lead you to the same place twice. In the Underworld, time and space are subjective and many people who have mapped the Underworld and tried to go back to the exact same time and place have been disappointed to find themselves in an unexpected location. I find this to be one of the beautiful and mysterious qualities of the Underworld. It is an interesting concept to explore.

The skull can be used to summon dark and malicious spirits that you can use to curse and bring death to your enemies. This is something I would never teach to students or anyone who asked. I do think it is important to know that it is possible; not all magick is friendly. It is also important to remember that just because you have ethics and honor does not mean that your enemies do. It is important to understand that dark spirits can be summoned with the skull.

One question I am often asked is if one must obtain a real human skull. The answer is no, you do not. Remember, power and magick come from the magician and not from the tools. Tools are there to help us when we are learning and the more adept and powerful you become, the less you will need to rely on your magical tools. You may use a skull replica or an artistic skull sculpture. I suggest using a skull that closely resembles a real human skull in the beginning. This will create the necessary spiritual link in your mind and energy field to do this kind of spiritual work.

The Celts practiced ancestor worship. This took a variety of forms. First and foremost, they believed that the dead existed among us and could easily be contacted. Some Celts believed that their Ancestors were directly descended from the gods. The Celts were headhunters. They believed that the souls resided in, and could be summoned back into, the skulls of the dead. They believed that the more heads a warrior collected, the more access to the spirits of the dead they had. This was done mostly to their enemies in war. The spirits of the slain warriors could be summoned back with magick and used as oracles and divination. To most modern people, this sounds very strange and very much like a form of "black magick." But, in ancient times, people had a different way of life and different ethics. One such ancient Celtic belief was that it was completely justified to use magick against someone if they threatened the survival of the tribe. Times were tough and sometimes cruel, and the way they viewed survival was different from how we view survival. The skulls of the dead helped the Celts with prophecies such as if an enemy was planning attack, harsh weather coming, or if spirits where working against them. These are only a few things talking heads could be used for. As we can see, having them gave the Celts an advantage for survival.

The Skull Meditation

1. Obtain a skull or skull replica.
2. Place it on your lap or on a small table in front of you.

3. Turn off all the lights. You may have a small candle nearby, but the room should be very dim.

4. Gaze upon the skull and allow any thoughts about the image or of death to come to mind.

5. Take a deep breath and allow those thoughts to fade away with each exhale.

6. Now, think about your spirit. It is the part of you that will never die. Your spirit can never be destroyed.

7. Know that the skull is a representation of your spirit. The spirit is your pure essence. It is that which is beyond time and space.

8. Continue to gaze upon the skull. How do you feel? What fears or hopes come to mind?

9. Now place your fingers on your head and feel your own skull. Feel the eye sockets, the nose bones, the cheekbones, the cranium, and the jawbone. Your skull is not your literal spirit, but it is a symbol of your spirit. Keep this in mind as you feel your own skull. What sensations do you feel? What insights pop up in your mind?

10. Journal about your experience.

Initiation of the Bones (Skeleton Meditation)

When working with the Underworld and the Ancestors, it is important for us to understand our inner nature and our core being. The spirit can often feel unfathomable for magical practitioners. We hear about the spirit from members of clergy in different religions and from books about spiritual enlightenment. But we cannot learn about the spirit through books and simply being a "good person." Our spirit is much more vast, complex, and timeless than we can understand. There also may be some confusion about the difference between the soul and the spirit. In patriarchal religions there is often a lot of talk about saving the soul and what happens to the soul after death. The spirit is our core being: that which survives after death and even after the soul is gone. The spirit is our pure light of self. I use the term "light" because we tend to think of white light as pure and universal, that which is unchanging and unwavering. People with psychic vision often report spirits and benevolent beings looking like white light. I believe that the spirit can be that, but it is much more. Something to contemplate: Perhaps these ascended beings appear to us as white light because the true nature of spirit is too complex for our eyes and minds to understand.

The soul is the part of our selves that houses the spirit. While the spirit is the pure essence of our spiritual being, the soul is everything that makes you *you* in this life. Your soul contains your ego, hopes and fears, dreams and desires, and your memories. The spirit is unbreakable and resilient, but the soul is at times fragile and can easily break away from us. This is why shamanic soul retrieval exists. When we experience a tragedy or accident, sometimes the great psychological and/or emotional impact can be too much for our soul to handle, so a part of our soul "breaks" off and flees to another part of the three worlds. Depending upon the personality of the event, psycho-emotional factors, and other external circumstances, the soul can journey anywhere in the three worlds to hide, heal, and regroup. One of the duties of the shaman is to find the soul fragment and bring it back to us to help us reintegrate it into our being. The soul's purpose is to help us learn, evolve, and become higher beings in our own right. I like to think of the soul as an intermediary between our spirit and our astral selves.

When working with the dead, it is imperative to begin the process for understanding our divine nature. Often, the ego of the shaman, witch, and magician gets in the way of their spiritual work and they begin to do it for the wrong reasons. This is not to say that when this happens the shaman is evil or bad, it is just to say that they have strayed from their divine purpose for that moment and need guidance. I have seen magicians who summon and work with the dead simply for ego-based reasons including power, greed, and arrogance. These things have no place when working with the Ancestors or any concept of the divine. To understand our spirit and our divine will we need to contemplate and meditate with our seemingly ineffable spirit.

As we have learned, to the ancient peoples the bones of our skeleton represented the unchanging and undying spirit. Bones are magical and resilient. They represent our divine selves. One way to meditate with our own spirit is to meditate on our own bones.

1. Sit or lie down and make yourself comfortable.
2. Take a deep breath and with the exhale allow your mind to relax.
3. Take another deep breath and with the exhale allow your emotions to find balance.
4. With one more deep breath, as you exhale allow all the muscles in your body to relax.
5. Close your eyes and visualize your body. See yourself exactly as you appear now.
6. After a moment, visualize the inside of your body. See your muscles, organs, nerves, veins, etc. Now, let that visualization fade away until you can see nothing but your bones. Know that your bones are powerful, unchanging, undying. This is your spirit. These are the bones of your Ancestors. These are the bones of your family for the generations to come.

7. See your bones becoming bright light. Watch them become brighter. Spend some time contemplating the bright spirit light of the bones. How does this make you feel? What insight do you get? What wisdom do you learn from the bones?

8. When you are ready, open your eyes, take a deep breath, stretch, and then journal about your experience.

Gravestones

The gravestone is an important tool when working with the dead. At the most basic level it acts as a grave marker. It lets us know where a corpse lies, the name of the deceased, and the dates of birth and death. On a magical level, it keeps the spirit of the deceased right where they are. People in the past used to fear that the spirit of the dead might journey out of the grave to haunt the nearby village. At worst, they may have feared that the body would be reanimated, get out of the grave, and walk around like a modern-day version of a zombie or a vampire. The magical powers of the stone and prayers said around it acted as a spiritual weight that prevented the spirit and the corpse from leaving the grave and running amok.

In necromancy and spirit work, the gravestone can be used for a couple of different purposes. First, it can be used as a temporary vessel for a spirit when you conjure them out of the grave. It is sometimes easier for the spirit of the dead to manifest if it has a vessel of some kind that it can use temporarily to commune with us. A magician would use the vessel during a necromantic ritual. After the rite was over the magician would dismiss the spirit and magically cleanse the gravestone. Another use for gravestones is as portals to different places in the Underworld while in the astral.

Oracles and Guides

The dead can be used as oracles. They have the ability to see the workings of time and space and they may be able to help you in seeing the past, present, and future. In the beginning during your practice, use your own Ancestors for oracle work. This may take some time at first, but with training and help from you and other Ancestors, they will be able to become quite proficient. When you become comfortable using the dead for oracle work, then you may use other willing spirits of the dead. It is better to use spirits that you know or who were magical in life. Sometimes spirits that we do not know will want offerings and libations and will tell you what they think you want to hear. Over time, you will be able to tell who is telling you the truth and who is not. For now, stick with your Ancestors and ask your ancestral teacher the best way to help your own Ancestors learn oracle work.

Blood Magick

Blood magick is important in the magick and use of the Underworld. It is through the power of blood that we are able to communicate more efficiently with the dead and learn about our Ancestors. Blood carries our life essence and our DNA. In Traditional Chinese Medicine it carries our Chi and in Ayurvedic Medicine it carries our Prana. Our blood literally is our life force. It is the liquid substance that carries information about every part of our physical and spiritual makeup. Blood is one of the transportation systems of our body, delivering vital information and nutrients to our organs and bones. It also can carry infection and disease to our bodies. The same blood that flows through our veins is the same blood that flowed through the veins of our Ancestors.

In magick, blood holds both power and taboo in its use. The ancients knew of the magical powers and abilities of blood. They knew that blood had a life-giving power. There are several theories about how this came to be. One theory states that the ancients saw how people died if they had no blood and so they knew that blood was the substance that gave life. Another theory says that as blood was spilled on the Earth, the ancients saw how it helped plants grow stronger. Modern scientists say that it was simply the nutrients in the blood fertilizing the Earth, but shamans, witches, and magicians know it is more than this. We know that not only does blood contain nutrients, but it also carries our energetic life force. The ancient pagans used blood in sacrifice. It is for this reason that Judeo-Christian magicians would place great taboos and warnings on the use of blood in magick. They would teach that blood was used to conjure demons and steer the magician down the dark path of black magick. While I will say you can use blood in black magick you can also use blood in healing and ancestral magick.

Sometimes the ancients used their own in a blood-letting ritual and other times it was animal and/or human sacrifice. "Sacrifice" is a word that sometimes inspires caution in the Neopagan and New Age practitioner. They much prefer the idea of "offering" to the cold sound of "sacrifice." But we need to be clear. To give sacrifice is to give something up of yourself or something that you own. Take a moment to think about it. When someone gives you an offering, they are giving you something that they can easily obtain. But when someone gives a sacrifice to you, they are giving you something that has great meaning to them. In turn, they give it more spiritual power because of the importance of the object. So, receiving the sacrifice carries more energy to you. It is also important to remember that when you give sacrifice to a spirit or entity, you must do it because you want to do it and never give sacrifice begrudgingly. Think about times in your life you knew someone gave you something, not because they wanted to, but because they felt they had to. It takes the specialness out of the item and you do not want it as much.

Sacrifice in the ancient past was common. The Maya gave human sacrifice to their gods. More specifically, they gave the blood and the heart of the victim to the gods so that they could manifest their powers more efficiently on the Earth. When the Maya gave sacrifice, it was not because they were bloodthirsty, but because they believed it would help the cycles of the crops, the community, and the Earth continue to thrive. The Celts also sacrificed humans for the same reasons. Some scholars say that the ancient tribes of Palestine sacrificed humans to their gods, but as time progressed, animal sacrifice was substituted. This may be the meaning behind the story in Genesis of Abraham preparing to sacrifice his son Isaac before seeing the ram caught in the bush. The Greco-Romans commonly gave animal sacrifice to the gods. Before and after a successful hunt, the hunters would give a portion of the kill to the Goddess of the Hunt, Artemis/Diana. It was also common to keep goats in the temple of Artemis/Diana so that the priests could give blood sacrifice to the goddess to win her favors. However, there were also times when the pagan gods would demand human sacrifice to keep the spirit of that person close to them. It is important to remember that the ancient pagan gods meant everything to the community and the individual person. It was common for mortals to be literally *in love* with their chosen patron or matron. To give your life to your god and eternally be by their side was, at one time, considered an honor.

Sometimes we may get upset when we hear or read that the gods demanded human or animal sacrifice. We may think that this is a cosmically "unfair" act because we are lesser beings than the gods. Yet it is important to realize that the gods experience this phenomenon too. In myth, we see that the gods were also sacrificed for the greater good of the cosmos.

Osiris was killed by his brother Set and sent to the Underworld. Because of this, Osiris is able to aid the newly dead through the labyrinth of the Dwat and help them join with the gods. Asclepius, the Greco-Roman god of healing, is killed by Jupiter/Zeus and then later exalted to godhood by his father Apollo. This enables him to have greater powers to help heal mankind. In Christian myth, Jesus is sacrificed on the cross to save mankind from sin and allow the souls of the dead to dwell in heaven. Ancient peoples believed that the universe did not have an inexhaustible amount of energy. When the universe needed to evolve to something greater it needed a large amount of energy to do so. By sacrificing the gods themselves this provided the energy needed.

The Blood of Creation (Maya)

There was only the darkness of the void. Before time, there was no time. Before space, there was no space. Before creation, there was nothingness. The first beings gathered together in a circle. They knew of themselves and they soon came to know each other. But the void remained. There was still nothingness. Their power was vast and unimaginable, but it was contained. The power of all things was contained inside their bodies. The gods had come together to begin creation and creation would be released from within them.

The gods fashioned a sharp dagger made of their own bones. The bones of the first gods formed the very core of the beginning of what was soon to come. Creation. But there needed to be more. The power within must be released. The gods took the sharp daggers and raised them high above their heads. They looked each other in the eye. Their minds were joined now. Their thoughts the same. Creation. In unison, the gods plunged the sharp daggers through their penises! Agonizing blood spilled out into the void. The power was released. The blood spilled into the nothingness and began creation. The cosmos was forming out of the drops of painful blood that spilled from the penises of the gods. The cosmos formed other gods; the other gods formed the Earth, sea, and sky. The raw power of the blood from those great penises contained the essence of fire and creation. The new gods took the blood and continued to create the universe. The very DNA of all things was made from the DNA of the great gods. Creation continues from the blood of the old ones.

If we look closely at this myth, we can take the story and learn to use blood magick ourselves. Blood can create life and add great power to our magick. When we use blood in magick it puts our astral and energetic signature on magical work that we are doing. When using blood magick it is vital that no one other than you handle or have care of the items that contain your blood. Your blood is one of the most powerful energetic ways to link back to you. A magician could potentially use the item with your blood against you. Never allow this to happen.

Witchblood

Anyone who has studied Traditional Witch lore has heard of the term *witchblood*. This means a person who comes from a hereditary witch family. This does not have to be direct lineage from the immediate family such as father to son or mother to daughter. If there was a magical person in your family several generations back, it may be that the magical energy skipped a few generations before manifesting in you. If so, you may still have the witchblood. I have heard some modern witches, shamans, and magicians say that if you go back through your ancestral lineage far enough you will find someone with witchblood because everyone in ancient times was a witch, shaman, or magician. Let me tell you that this is not true. First, let me explain what a witch really is. Neopagans use a modern interpretation of the word witch. Today, the word witch can mean anyone who follows a magical or spiritual path and works with the energy of the Universe. In ancient times witch meant anyone, be they Christian, pagan, or any religion who worked with the primal, darker forces of the Universe to obtain a desired goal. This could mean cursing, working with the dead, conjuring demons, or healing. They also summoned chthonic powers and spirits to benefit the community such as for weather working and to provide food for the tribe. Most modern witches would be aghast that I said such a thing, but it is true. There is nothing wrong with redefining a word, but it is important to know where the word came from and what it originally meant. Not every human in the far distant past was a magician, witch, or shaman. These were and are very specialized skills that use specific energies for the purpose of the conjurer. Many people who are witches believe that they have a distant relative who was a witch and the magick has passed down to them. I believe that this is perfectly fine to believe whether it is true or not. I look at it this way, if it makes your magick and spirituality more meaningful, then why not?

So how does witchblood work? The witchblood is like a spiritual calling card between you, your Ancestors, and the gods. The blood sometimes "boils" with magick and power. When one has "the blood", as it is sometimes called, a person cannot ignore the spiritual call of the ancient ones and the shining ones. To do so usually ends in psychosis and madness. I think of it as a genetic energy power surge that, if used, has the potential to help humanity reconnect with the three worlds. Not everyone has the witchblood. This does not mean that if you do not feel the fire in the blood that you are not a witch, magician, or shaman. This means that the magical blood begins with you. If you are the first in your family line to be a witch, then great! You may have just as much power as someone who is from a family of witches. Think of it this way: just because you do not come from a family of doctors does not mean you will not be a skilled doctor once you receive medical training.

Hyndla and Freya (Norse)

The goddess Freya went to the dark cave of the giantess Hyndla. She knew that Hyndla was a seeress and knew how to use her magick to see the Ancestors of everyone in the Nine Worlds. Freya promised the giantess that if she would grant her a favor, she could convince the great gods Odin and Thor to grant blessings on her. Reluctantly, Hyndla came out of her dark cave. Hyndla wanted nothing more but to slumber in the darkness of the Earth. Freya appealed to the giantess to come with her. Hyndla agreed. She rode off on her wolf and Freya on her magical boar. However, Hyndla could not be fooled. She knew that Freya, the goddess of love, rode no ordinary boar. The boar she rode was her lover, Ottar, who was transformed into the animal. Yet Freya protested; she tried to convince the giantess that her boar was not her lover in disguise.

Freya asked the giantess about the lineage of Ottar. Hyndla knew Freya was up to something. The gods do not often make friends with the giants so easily. She decided to give Freya what she had asked for. She used her magick to tap into the blood of Ottar. Through magick of the blood, she could see deep into his family history. She could see deeper than all other beings in the Nine Worlds. She began naming off Ottar's lineage. She named the names of men that were long forgotten by time. She named those who deeds were legendary. She named those who may have wanted to keep themselves secret, even from the gods!

Freya was happy to hear the family names of Ottar. She told Hyndla to give Ottar the magick potion that would make him remember all that he had heard. Hyndla knew Freya was up to something. There would be no reward or treasures for this. She then told the goddess that if Ottar drinks the potion it would do nothing but curse him. Freya feared not. With her own magick she would make sure the potion Ottar drank held no curse. With this, Hyndla returned to her cave to slumber ever deep.

Tapping into the Blood

As we can see from the story above, there is magick in our blood. Our blood contains every bit of information about our past, present, and even future. It has the DNA of our Ancestors. The blood that ran through your forefathers runs through you. Our blood can tell you the state of your current health as well as possible future troubles not yet detected. On a spiritual and energetic level, our blood contains many magical abilities. There are several legends about the bloodline of shamans, witches, magicians, and healers. When we say that magick "runs in the family", we are specifically referring to the power that is transferred to each generation through the bloodline. It is thought that the Ancestors and gods of the ancient past run in the blood as well. To access this deep, powerful magick, all we have to do is connect on an energetic and spiritual level to the blood. This can be done quite easily.

Exercise: Tapping into the Blood

1. Relax your body and take full slow breaths.
2. Bring your awareness to a meditative trance state.
3. Bring your attention to your heart. Feel the heart pumping blood to your entire body.
4. Become aware of the arteries and veins that make up the circulatory system of your body. This is the lifeblood that pumps within you.
5. Understand that the same blood that pumps through your body

also pumped through the bodies of your parents, your grandparents, your great-grand parents, and back to the beginning of the human race.

6. As you focus on your blood, take a breath and breathe in life force form the air. I like to visualize it a vibrant gold or orange color. See the life force enliven and awaken your blood. Visualize your blood glowing red like embers or lava from deep within the Earth. Your blood becomes enlivened from this energy.

7. Think about your Ancestors. Think about your family lineage throughout all of human history.

8. Call to your Ancestors. Ask them to be present within and around you. Feel the power of the blood give your ancestors energy to manifest in the physical plane.

9. Bring to mind the Ancestors you wish to speak to and have a deeper connection with. Think about what they look like and sound like if you know.

10. Connect with your ancestral altar. Touch it. Visualize all the Ancestors you work with holding hands with each other. Visualize them holding your hands. You and your Ancestors are forming a circle.

11. Take a deep breath and breathe the lifeforce to your Ancestors once again. See an energetic cord or line going to each one of them. Know that you are giving each other power and magick. The Ancestors are your past, and you are their future.

Journeying To The Blood

With this technique you will be taking a shamanic journey into the blood itself to speak with your ancestors. So, instead of journeying up or down the shamanic world tree, you will be using your blood as a catalyst to speak with your Ancestors that you already know, or you may use this technique to discover Ancestors from the distant past long forgotten. I enjoy using this technique to learn more about my ancestral heritage and the long-forgotten stories of my Ancestors.

1. Lie down or sit comfortably in a chair. Relax your body and take full slow breaths. State your purpose of seeing Ancestors known or unknown.

2. Bring your awareness to a meditative trance state. You may simply take nice deep hypnotic breaths if you like. With each breath allow yourself to go deeper and deeper into trance.

3. Bring your attention to your heart. Feel the heart pumping blood to your entire body.

4. Become aware of the arteries and veins that make up the circulatory system of your body. This is the lifeblood that pumps within you.

5. Have a deep understanding that the same blood that pumps through your body also pumped through the bodies of your parents, your grandparents, your great-grand parents, and back to the beginning of the human race.

6. Bring your awareness into your body; into your heart. Visualize yourself inside your own body inside the blood that pumps through the heart. What do you see?

7. With the powers of your visualization, journey deeper within the

DNA and Matrix of the blood. The DNA is a portal to your ancestors and those who share your bloodline in the future. Visualize yourself journeying into a magical energetic realm inside the blood. You may see people, places of the past, or some other magical place.

8. Visualize a place to meet your Ancestors or guides. You may see them somewhere in the Underworld, the astral plane, or perhaps somewhere in the history of your Ancestors.

9. When you see your Ancestors, greet them as you would any guest and speak with them for a while. When you are ready, say your goodbyes and bring your awareness back to your physical body and the physical plane.

10. Journal about your experience.

Blood in Magick and Necromancy

It is believed that one of the most powerful ways to empower something with magick is to use blood. Blood keeps us alive and has our life force and the DNA of our Ancestors. Blood carries the powers of the magician and witch. Everything we are and everything we hope to achieve is in our blood. We often hear people say: "It's in his blood!" Blood carries the components to heal our wounds and bring us back from sickness to health. To give something blood is to give it life and manifestation.

In necromancy, blood is a powerful way to summon spirits of the dead. Offerings of food, wine, and water help the dead manifest on the physical plane, but blood will give them the life force that they need to truly manifest on the physical plane and cause change. The spirits of the dead sometimes crave it. Its power can be seductive to them. In many cultures, the blood of the gods created life on Earth, and it is that same blood that can resurrect spirits of the dead, even temporarily. In Greco-Roman necromancy, blood was poured into a hole dug into the ground which became a doorway into Hades. The blood would give the dead power and life force and the necromancer was able to ask the spirit of the dead advice and wisdom of the Underworld. The Nordics would empower the runes with blood to magically charge them. When this was done, the runes were alive with power, ready to do magick. Oaths were sometimes signed with blood. This would magically bind the person to their oath forever. In medieval magick, blood is sometimes considered black magick because of the idea that blood was used to feed demons and a witch's pact with the devil was signed in blood. In Vodou and some African indigenous religions, blood from animals such as goats, chickens, and small animals is sometimes used to give devotion and energy to certain gods. Shamans and Neopagans may give a drop or two of their own blood to the spirit of a tree or plant as payment for harvesting the plant.

I personally feel that if a magical person understands themselves and the magick at hand and takes full responsibility of the magick being performed, then "do what ye will." Blood magick is an ancient magical practice and very powerful. In my personal practice, I believe that anytime blood is used in magick it binds you to the spell or ritual in a strong and powerful way. This can be a blessing or a curse. Some pagans use their blood to bind themselves to ancestral lands. The sweat and blood of their Ancestors worked the land and harvested food and shelter, so magically they want to bind their magick to the land to strengthen their ties to it and help the spirits of the place prosper. It can become a curse if you decide to bind a love spell with your blood. This connection is powerful and is seductive to the obsessed lover, but if the love affair becomes sour or should end for a variety of reasons, then ending the spell is very difficult.

Mayan Ancestral Blood Summoning Ritual

I mentioned the bloodthirst rites of the ancient Maya earlier and their interesting way of summoning the Ancestors. To the Mayans, the Ancestors had the power to influence magick, tell the future, heal, and cause harm to others to protect the family or the tribe. To summon the Ancestors, they would put paper or wood shavings into a sacred bowl. They then would take a large bone needle and pierce their penis if they were men or their tongue if they were women. They would then let the blood drip over the paper in the sacred bowl and allow it to dry. Once the blood had dried, they would ignite the paper on fire and summon the Ancestors for magick.

To modernize this ritual, you may obtain a sacred bowl or small cauldron and place wood shavings inside. Then make a mixture of incense using dittany of Crete, dragon's blood, and a couple of drops of your own blood. Place the mixture on the wood chips and allow them to burn. You may also skip the wood chips and place the incense on non-toxic charcoal instead [charcoal can generate more carbon monoxide than woodchips – so be careful in enclosed space]. The kind used for hookahs works well. Once the smoke begins to rise, you may use a conjuration such as:

> "I call upon my Ancestors (Ancestors' names)! Use this sacred smoke to draw energy and manifest yourself through the smoke and appear before me!"

You may adapt the words to your liking. The important thing is to let the Ancestors know that they can use the incense to manifest through the smoke to take shape. This may be challenging for your Ancestors if you have not been working with them for long. Remember, the Maya pierced themselves in the places of creation (penis) and manifestation (tongue the spoken word). I strongly recommend against performing this ritual in the traditional Mayan way. However, it is up to you to take responsibility for your own safety and well-being.

Spellcasting Using Blood

Using blood in magick is a very ancient practice. I remember when I was first learning, a friend told me that if you signed your spell with your name in blood, the spell or person you placed the spell on was forever bound to you. Honestly, that may or may not be true. I feel that if you believe that it is true, then perhaps your belief makes it so. Blood in magick also has the reputation from the old witch-hunt fears that if you use blood in magick then you are attracting evil forces. That is not necessarily true. If you choose to use blood in magick, the devil will not appear and make you sell your soul. That is purely a superstitious Christian belief. But as we have learned, blood contains a powerful life force and the DNA of the person or animal it originates from. Life force has an enormous amount of energy, and spirits use energy as food. I leave it up to you to choose to use a few drops of your own blood for magick. I have friends and colleagues who practice the religion of Vodou and use animal blood in their devotions and rituals. It may seem cruel and barbaric, but I am fond of reminding meat eaters that it is more sacred to use a chicken for magick and devotion than it is to keep it in a farm where its beak is cut short, it is given horrible hormones, and forced to live in its own feces.

Blood is sometimes given to one's gods and goddesses as a form of devotion and to strengthen the bond. To give of one's own blood to a god is a very sacred act. You are giving your very essence and life force. This should only be done to one's patron or matron. These are the gods and goddesses that you will work with for the rest of your life and the lifetimes to come. I personally work with other gods that are not my patron and matron and feel it is important to give to any gods that aid me in my spiritual growth devotion and offerings. However, I would never give those gods my own blood. The sharing of blood is a sacred act between my lifetime gods and myself. Another reason I don't share my blood with gods other than my matron or patron, is that I do not want just any god laying claim to me simply because they want my energy. This, to me, is vampirism.

When it comes to spirits and entities, especially demons and beings you do not know, you should not give them your, or anyone else's, blood under any circumstances. There are some grimoires that say to conjure certain spirits you should give them animal blood and/or human blood sacrifice. This is an unbelievably bad idea. First and foremost, to give them your own blood attaches them directly to you making them extremely difficult to banish. They also get a lot of energy from the blood, and they will no longer want other offerings. If you have a spirit that promises you power, love, or money in exchange for blood offerings, you should refuse! These are usually trickster and malicious spirits that have no real power of their own. The only way they can manifest your desire is to give them a power surge of blood. It is much easier to manifest your desires with devotions to a god or goddess.

Using bones and blood are the most powerful tools to use in magick. It is life. It is power. It is also makes an imprint on our consciousness and in the spirit world. These tools give spirits more power to manifest our will. They are most likely the first tools of magick and witchcraft. When we use these tools with reverence for their power, we tap into an ancient lineage of magick that goes all the way back to the first practitioner of necromancy and spirit work.

6
Magical Protection

When traveling in the Underworld or summoning its energies and entities, there is always a chance that something unwanted may follow you back to this world. It happens to the best of magicians. It is always a good idea to know some basic magical defense and protection. It is wise to remember that as human beings, we have more influence in the physical plane than most spirits do. You may come across powerful entities that become interested in you. Most are harmless and are simply curious about you and the magical talent that you possess. Some entities may see the life force within you and may be attracted to that energy. The Underworld is a place of the dead, demons, chthonic entities, and many things that we do not want to remain in the physical plane. If we are to work with the energies of the Underworld, then it is our responsibility to make sure that we put back anything that manifests on this plane because of us!

To protect ourselves and our temple space from Underworld entities, the first thing we must do is to makes sure that we treat all spirits with respect. If the being is grotesque and scary, we must still treat it with kindness. Sometimes spirits appear in your temple space unexpectedly because you may have opened a portal to their world. Being respectful brings you allies and equal respect from other spirits. If a spirit seems hostile to you there are a few things that you can do to send them back to where they belong.

Talking to the Spirit

The first thing you should always do with a spirit is to talk with it and find out what it wants. If you cannot hear what it says or it communicates in a different language, use your intuition. Pay attention to your feelings. What images pop up in your mind? Do you "know" what the spirit wants? Sometimes, the spirit may recognize something special in you and want a working relationship. But if it feels sinister, dark, or even evil, the best course of action is to ask it to leave. If that does not work, a more aggressive course of action is required. In the case of a hostile spirit, never allow the entity to remain in your home or temple space. The longer it is there, the harder it is to get rid of.

The Broom or Besom

The witch's broom conveys to us the idea of magical power. We have all seen the depictions of witches flying to the Sabbat on a broom. The broom has many mysteries, but for our purposes here we will talk about the broom's ability to cleanse and banish unwanted spirits and energies. As with all magical tools, our broom needs to be set aside from our everyday household sweeping. It should be cared for as a sacred magical tool and placed in a position of honor by your altar or sacred space. When you hold your broom, know that you are holding a powerful tool that has an ancestral lineage into the European past. Witches used this tool to heal and to protect. The bristles sweep away negative energies and spirits. Use the broom to sweep these out of your ritual space. Walk counterclockwise as you sweep. This is counter sunwise or widdershins, so it is ideal for banishing energies. Walk counterclockwise three times while sweeping the energies and negative spirits away. Visualize the negative energy being swept away into the Underworld to be recycled into something more productive and useful for the Earth. You may also sweep away negative spirits who threaten you. If you place your broom in front of a door, window, or portal, it acts as a barrier. No spirit can get through.

Blast of Power

Emotions are a great storehouse of energy. A blast of emotional power can banish an entity in a pinch. The trick is to summon a feeling of great control over your environment and a dire need for the spirit to be thrown out of your home. Think of it like a security guard throwing a thief out the door! It will not work if your fear outweighs your feeling of control. Negative spirits feed on the energy of fear. All you must do is build up this great emotion of control and aggression. Then wave your hand in the direction you want the spirit to go and say, "Go!" Remember, this is a temporary fix. After the blast of power, you must set up wards to keep the spirit from returning.

Wards

One of the best ways to keep unwanted spirits away from your home is to set up wards. A ward is focused energy that holds the intent of protection and keeping unwanted energies away from a person, place, or thing. The more common wards are written symbols (be they astrally or physically written) or physical objects that are magically charged. Some common symbols include: the pentacle, the equal-armed cross, reiki signs, god symbols, family or clan shields, or runes. You can make a simple ward by binding two rowan sticks together with red string to form an equal-armed cross. If hung over the window or rafters, it offers wonderful protection. You may also want to trace the *Elhaz* rune over doors, windows, and the four corners of your home. This is extremely effective, and I use this particular ward myself every day. Feel free to come up with your own symbols or glyphs that feel powerful and protective to you.

Banishing Without Prejudice

A powerful way to banish spirits energetically is to use the pentacle. You may take a magical athame, sword, dagger, or simply your index finger and trace a large flaming blue pentacle in the air. Begin toward your left knee, as you trace the pentacle, visualize it as a flaming blue line, and trace up above your head. Then trace the line to your right knee. Continue tracing over to your left shoulder, then straight across to your right shoulder, then trace the line back down to your left knee so that it connects with your starting point. You should see a large star of blue flame in front of you. Take your dagger or index finger and summon pure white divine light from the heavens into your dagger or finger. Then take a deep breath and on the exhale, forcefully send a beam of that divine light through the center of the pentacle while at the same time shouting "Go!" or "Begone!" Visualize every aspect and molecule of the spirit instantly disappearing. There should be no debris whatsoever.

Laughing

One of the most effective ways to get rid of a negative spirit is by laughing. As silly as it sounds, it works! Remember that negative spirits feed on the great power of fear. If we are laughing, then we ground our fears and transmute them into joy! The spirit is quickly deflated and has little to no influence in this world. It's one of the easiest ways to banish unwanted guests.

The Magical Ring

A magical ring is any ring that is consecrated with the intent of magick and protection. The ring can be silver, gold, copper, or iron. Silver summons the powers of the moon and can aid you with your psychic powers. Gold summons the powers of the sun. In Underworld magick, the sun can disperse negative energies and spirits and control demons. Copper has power over the dead. In Greco-Roman myths, copper was used to summon, control, and banish the dead. Iron is a metal that disperses spiritual energies. Only use iron to rid yourself and your space of negative energies. Other spirits do not like iron as much, so be careful and judicious with your use of iron implements. If you use a ring with a gemstone, make sure it is a stone of the sun such as heliotrope, tiger's eye, or sunstone. Sun energies help banish negative spirits.

Herbs/Crystals/Stones

Herbs have been used to protect people from negative magick and spirits for thousands of years! Different herbs have different energy signatures and spirits. Here are a few herbs that are easily obtainable from magical shops or online:

Sage - used to purify and protect

Osha Root - banishes negative/evil spirits

Frankincense - purification, exorcism, banishing

Rue - protection, banishes negative energy placed upon you

Rosemary - purification and cleansing

Onion - absorbs negative energy, can be placed in windows as a ward against evil

Lemon - very powerful plant. Lemon juice can be put in blessed water for purification of the body, home, magical tools, etc.

Lemon grass & Lemon Verbena - purification herbs. Can be used similar to lemon.

Quartz crystal - can be empowered with protective energy and spells. Quartz can be placed in a circle and charged forming a powerful protective circle or barrier.

Salt - grounds energies. Salt has a powerful "draining" effect on spirits. It can quickly diminish their power in the Middleworld.

Tiger's Eye - ruled by the sun. It has a powerful banishing and deflecting effect against negative energies.

Sunstone - powerful solar energies. Used to "frighten" negative spirits. The solar powers of the stone banish spirits and diminishes their influence in our world.

Coscaria - ground eggshells make a powerful protective barrier around you and your home. Placed on the back of the neck it defends against possessions.

Camphor - more of a chemical than an herb, but spirits do not like the toxicity. It has draining effect on spirits.

Bloodstone (heliotrope) - controls and banishes negative spirits.

Red Brick - made simply by powdering a red brick. Can be used to Dust "seal" or "wall" something out. Keeps negative forces away.

Vinegar - Keeps negative energy and spirits away. More natural than chemicals. Be cautious because it also keeps good and healing spirits away as well.

Chemicals

These are not healthy for the environment, but if needed, household cleansers such as Ajax, Lysol, and Pine Sol can quickly banish spirits.

Ammonia (in small doses) works well too. Spirits become quickly drained when a generous amount of cleansers are around. Their astral essence quickly dissipates. Do not use chemicals against spirits except as a last resort. Using chemicals to banish all the time can result in other spirits not wanting to work with you. Also, be aware that if there are any spirit allies in your temple it will have the same effect on them.

Incense and Fumigations

A wonderful way to keep unwanted spirits from your home or temple is to purify with incense and fumigations. A fumigation is simply an archaic term meaning the act of using incense to cleanse the space. One common way is to smudge your ritual space and your entire home, with sage or mugwort. You may also use a combination of any herb that is used to protect, purify, and banish. Just place your mixture on a charcoal briquette and let the fumes do their magick. Two good books I referenced before for this are Scott Cunningham's *Oil's, Incense, and Brews* and Judika Illes' *The Element Encyclopedia of 5000 Spells*.

Ancestor Magick

The Ancestors can provide a powerful defense against unwanted entities. They have a great amount of influence in both this world and the Underworld. However, you must work with them for a while to build up their power in this world. One way Ancestors can help is to use their energy and influence to escort the spirit away. They may also call upon a higher Underworld spirit to help with this. If a trickster spirit is in my home, I place my hands upon the ancestral altar. I visualize my Ancestors and myself holding hands in a circle. I then visualize brilliant white light forming a powerful sphere all around us. This magick sphere banishes the trickster spirit back to where it came from.

God Magick

The gods we work with are the most powerful force against negative spirits. This, in addition to the wonderful sense of connectedness and love you feel, is one of the chief reasons why it is so important to work with a specific god and/or goddess and give them offerings and devotions. Whenever you feel threatened, do not be afraid to call your personal gods. They are invested in you as you are in them and will quickly come to your aid.

I personally try to handle negative spirits myself before I call upon my gods. They can provide a wonderful defense against negative spirits, but this privilege should not be abused. Do not think that because the gods have great power over spirits that you can be irresponsible when you conjure spirits of any sort. If you abuse the power of the gods, they may not come to your aid. I only call upon my gods to deal with negative spirits when I have exhausted all other avenues. You can, however, invoke their energies when you are performing a banishing. This allows you to tap into their powers without them having to do the work themselves.

Talismans/Charms/Medicine Bags

You can make protective charms and bags very easily. You simply take an herb or a stone and put magical energy in them with the intent of protecting you and your space, or banishing a spirit completely. Remember, there are some powerful spirits that will require more than a charm to banish them. Medicine bags can combine several different items. You may use stones, bones, herbs, coins, powders, or anything you can think that will protect you and your space!

You can make a talisman with things such as coins, jewelry, wood, necklaces, or any object that feels powerful to you. Here is an easy ritual to create and consecrate a protective talisman. It is best to perform during a waning or full moon.

> Items needed:
> Talisman
> Incense stick
> Candle
> Small bowel of water
> Salt

1. Find an object that feels magical to you. You may buy a protective talisman online or at a magick shop or you can simply look for stone or some other item that feels magical.
2. Place the talisman on your altar, the incense in the east, candle in the south, water in the west, and salt in the north.
3. State your intention to the spirits and gods of empowering and consecrating your protective talisman.
4. Purify with sage, the besom, or any purification herb you like.
5. If you like, you may draw your magical circle. Then, call to the four directions beginning with east (air), south (fire), west (water), and north (earth)
6. Place both hands over the talisman and send protective energies inside. Visualize yourself and your home being protected by pure magical energy.
7. Pass the talisman through the incense smoke and say: "I ask the spirits of air to protect my mind. Let no entity use my thoughts against me nor give me thoughts of doubt. May only mental clarity prevail!"

8. Pass the talisman through the candle flame (or above it if object is flammable) and say: "I ask the spirits of fire to protect my will. Let no entity make me question my purpose. May only my Divine Will prevail!"

9. Place the talisman into the water (or sprinkle a few drops on the talisman) and say: "I ask the spirits of water to protect my emotions. Let no entity use me emotions against me. May only emotional stability prevail!"

10. Place the talisman into the salt and say: "I ask the spirits of earth to protect my body. Let no entity cause me physical harm in any way. May only bodily strength and health prevail!"

11. Take your empowered talisman to the east. Face the east and visualize the air and the sylphs and say: "Sylphs, spirits of air. Bless and consecrate my talisman!" Visualize the yellow sylphs spinning around the east. See them go around and into your talisman giving it power and blessing.

12. Take your empowered talisman to the south. Face the south; visualize fire and the salamanders and say: "Salamanders, spirits of fire. Bless and consecrate my talisman!" Visualize the red salamanders spinning around the south. See them go around and into your talisman giving it power and blessing.

13. Take your talisman to the west. Face the west; visualize water and the undines and say: "Undines, spirits of water. Bless and consecrate my talisman!" Visualize blue undines spinning around the west. See them go around and into your talisman giving it power and blessing.

14. Take your talisman to the north. Face the north; visualize earth and

forest and the gnomes and say: "Gnomes, spirits of earth. Bless and consecrate my talisman!" Visualize the green gnomes spinning around the north. See them go around and into your talisman giving it power and blessing.

15. If you like, you may ask your god and/or goddess to bless your talisman. You may visualize the god/dess standing in front of you giving your talisman power, or you may visualize divine white light coming from above blessing your talisman.

16. Thank the spirits and each direction. In my spiritual tradition we don't banish or dismiss the elemental spirits because without them we could not exist. We simply say, "Thank you (name of spirit) for your work tonight. You are always welcome in the circle of my life."

17. Allow the power to absorb into the talisman. Keep it covered for a couple of days before use.

Mirrors

Mirrors can be used to scare or drive away negative spirits. If you hang a mirror in your window or outside your door it will reflect negative energy away. This also helps when someone is purposely sending negative magick at you as well. You can also hang multifaced glass crystals as well. These direct the energies to go away from your home.

Ritual to Banish Unwanted Spirits or Demons

You may use a formal ceremonial banishing ritual if you would like. This ritual will summon Kabbalistic energies to banish a spirit:

I. Banish

Perform the Lesser Banishing Ritual of the Pentagram. This will banish most negative energies and spirits and will clear the way for you to banish the more powerful spirits. Think of it like sweeping the floor before you mop it. Essentially, this is what you are doing astrally.

II. Circle

You will draw a circle or sphere that will protect you from any negative energies while you perform the ritual. Before you draw the circle, you will need to place a Triangle of Art or another device that will hold the spirit in place. You can use a clear quartz crystal if you like. Draw your circle using your tool of choice such as an athame, dagger, broom, or your index finger. Just remember to visualize your circle as a sphere or dome of flaming blue light through which no enemy or hostile entity can enter.

III. Archangels

At each of the four directions call the powers of the four Archangels. In the East is Raphael. In the South is Michael. The West is Gabriel. And the North is Ariel. You have already summoned the archangels in the Lesser Banishing Ritual of the Pentagram, but this will provide an anchor in your mind that your magical circle is protected by these mighty powers.

IV. Circumambulations/Raising Power

To raise power in your circle, walk clockwise fully around the circle (circumambulate) beating a drum or rattle. This will help you gather magical energy for your banishing.

V. Invoking Divine Power

To give your ritual added power, you may add the divine power of your god or goddess with which you work. If you do not work with a particular god or goddess, you may say a prayer to God or Goddess or The Creator. Ask the divine to give you blessings, protection, and to empower your banishing. Ask the divine to aide you in banishing the negative energy or spirit.

VI. Banishing

Now you are ready to banish the aggressive spirit.

A. The Command

You must command the spirit into the Triangle of Art or your quartz crystal. You must feel the power of the god or goddess coursing through your body. You must know that you have the powers of the Universe at your disposal.

You may use your own commands or use the one below.

"(Name of spirit) (if you do not know the name of the spirit just say "spirit"), by the power of (god/goddess) I command you into the Triangle of Art (or crystal)! You shall be bound within until I give you command to depart! In the name of (god/goddess), so be it!

Visualize the spirit manifesting into the Triangle of Art or the crystal. They cannot escape! You could skip this part if you feel that you do not need to contain the spirit, but the benefit of containing the spirit is that it allows the buildup of magick and spiritual power to hit the spirit all at once. You also have a focal point for the banishing.

"I command you (name of spirit) to depart this physical plane never to return. You shall return to the realm from whence you came, harming no one or thing upon your return. Depart! Depart! Depart, I say!"

You must say this command with extreme authority and force! You have the power of the gods behind you! You are a god in your temple space. As you say, so it is!

B. Banishing with prejudice

If the spirit has enough power to stay on the physical plane, even with your magical commands, then you may banish with extreme prejudice. Banishing with prejudice means that when you send energy to banish something you are doing it with full confidence and force that the energy or entity must be 100% destroyed. Do not do this with a spirit who has simply gotten lost and ended up in your temple space because of an accident for which you are responsible. Be respectful to the spirit but be firm. If a negative energy is trying to cause you harm and will not depart, then banish it without prejudice.

To do this, take your magical athame or dagger and point it towards the sky. Summon divine powerful white light into the blade. Aim it at the crystal or Triangle of Art. Take a deep breath and muster every ounce of magical force you have. Know that you wield the power of the gods! Then with a mighty yell, say, "GO!" or "Be gone!" and visualize the divine light striking the spirit like a laser beam. This beam evaporates the spirit. It is gone. It is banished back to the realm from which it came.

VII. Thanks and Ending the Rite

When you are ready, thank the spirits and gods that you have conjured. Begin by releasing the energies of the deity whom you have invoked. Be sure to thank them and offer them your love and blessings. Then, beginning in the North with Ariel, thank the archangels one by one and bid them farewell. Afterwards, dismantle your circle.

VIII. Banish

End the ritual with the Lesser Banishing Ritual of the Pentagram, smudge, or banish with your besom. This will get rid of any spirit debris or left over energies after your banishing ritual. If you have a favorite way you enjoy cleansing the ritual space you may use the technique of your choice.

Valediction

We have come to the end of the first part of our journey. We have journeyed deeper into the depth of the Underworld and death. It is natural to fear death. We want to live happy healthy lives and death is not what most of us want. We fear what we do not understand. It is my hope that you understand the process of death is part of the spiritual process. We must face our fears to release our truest potential. Even still, a healthy respect for death is programmed in our psyche to help us survive. There are those who romanticize the dark and shadowy aspects of the Universe. Some witches, shamans, and magicians may seek out the Angel of Death himself, but as we have learned, he is not the hellish figure from popular culture or even medieval depictions. The Angel of Death is a healer in his own way, taking the spirit away from the broken body to the world of the ancestors.

In this book, we covered how ancient pagans honored death in numerous ways. Among those ways, necromancy in some form was commonly used to communicate with the dead. In the Temples of the Dead in Greece and Rome, many travelers would enter the temples seeking yearning to speak with their beloved dead one last time. They believed that they were traveling into Hades and speaking with the shades of their loved one. I believe that this is a form of therapy for the living. When they communicated with the dead, they were able to make their peace and move on. The Egyptians, of course, took great pains in preserving the body after death because they believed that for the spirit to remain intact, the body must be intact. As we learned, one of the most sacred ceremonies in ancient Greece was the Eleusinian Mysteries teaching the seeker the mysteries of death and rebirth. The Lakota Ghost Dance summoned the ancestors during a sacred dance to ask for aid for the benefit of the tribe. We saw that many cultures believed the ancestors have the power to help their descendants with the things they need in life such as food, land disputes, and the governing of the people.

In modern paganism, it is important that we continue the practice of honoring our ancestors. We often honor our gods, but do not have a place in our spiritual practice for our sacred Ancestors. Having a shrine in our homes helps the Ancestors manifest in our magical practice and our daily lives. In Native American cosmology, the ancestors do not leave us for heaven or the Underworld, they remain here to help us on our spiritual path. When we honor them daily and give them offerings, they will gain the strength to aid us in our magick. But be patient. Unless your ancestors were magical, it may take them a little while to understand how magick works. If we stick with this practice, the Ancestors will learn as we learn and we can establish a fulfilling and powerful magical practice. They can even help us with healing ancestral or negative family patterns and sickness that manifest in our lives. This, to me, is one of the greatest aspects of healing.

Summoning the dead in ritual sometimes brings to mind nefarious magicians hellbent on doing dark magick, but the dead can be very helpful in magick. There are many places that will aide in spirit manifestations, such as cemeteries, mausoleums, and natural places like lakes and ponds. The dead can tell us prophecies, divination, wisdom, and help us to grieve when we summon a loved one. There are many myths that describe bringing the dead back to life. It takes an immense amount of power and usually it is usually the gods who can do this. Bringing back someone from the dead into a broken body is something we never want to do. When working with the dead in magick it is important to be respectful just as you would with any other spirit.

Working with the dead can help us understand our spiritual lineage in a deep way. Our ancestors can help us tap into the sacred magick of our blood lines. They can also help us learn about own spirit and the magick that we possess deep inside the core of our being. There are many tools such as the skull and bones that can help us tune into our deepest nature of spirit. At first glance these things may seem macabre, but our bones are as natural as the earth itself. When we truly understand the depths of our spirit, it is then we can connect to the spirit world to enhance our magick, deepen our understanding of the Universe, and continue our journey into the depths of the unknown.

These two volumes of *Underworld* have been a very enjoyable process for me, and I have gotten great joy in teaching the myths and magical techniques to shamans, witches, and pagans. This work is a culmination of my experience and research for the past 25 years. One of my spiritual goals is to help people to reconnect to the three shamanic worlds. The two volumes of *Underworld* are only part of the work that needs to be done for fuller understanding of the spiritual Universe.

Other Works

Now that you have explored the Underworld and learned to build extensive relationships with the Ancestors, be sure to continue your journey through the worlds with my other offerings. In *Upperworld: Shamanism and Magick of the Celestial Realms,* we journey to the Upperworld to discover the many ancient beings in the above worlds that can help us learn about the energies of the Universe and transform our lives for healing, power, and spiritual evolution.

Bibliography

Angels, Demons, and Gods of the New Millennium. Lon Milo Duquett. Weiser. 1997.

Alice In Wonderland. Lewis Carroll. Bantam classics. 1984.

American Indian Myths and Legends. Richard Erdoes and Alfanso Ortiz. Pantheon Books. 1984.

Aspects of Anglo-Saxon Magic. Bill Griffiths. Anglo-Saxon Books. 1996.

Bardo Teachings : *The Way of Death and Reburth.* Lama Lodu. Snow Lion Pub. 1982, 2010.

Becoming Osiris: The Ancient Egyptian Death Experience. Ruth Schumann Antelme and Stephane Rossini. Inner Traditions International. 1995.

The Book of Fallen Angels. Michael Howard. Capall Bann. 2004.

The Book of Solomon's Magick. Carroll "Poke" Runyon, M.A. The Church of Hermetic Sciences Inc. 1996.

British Witchcraft and Magic. Emma Wilby. Sussex Academy Press. 2005.

Call of the Horned Piper. Nigel Aldcroft Jackson. Capall Bann Publishing. 1994.

The Cup of Destiny. Trevor Ravenscroft. Weiser Books. 1982.

The Celtic Book of the Dead. Caitlin Matthews. Grange Books. 2001.

Communing With The Spirits. Martin Coleman. Samuel Wieser, Inc. 1998.

The Complete Book of Incense, Oils, and Brews. Scott Cunningham. Llewellyn Publications. 1989.

Courageous Dreaming. Alberto Villoldo, PH.D. Hay House Inc. 2008.

Cunning-Folk and Familiar Spirits: Shamanistic Visionary Traditions In Early Modern British Witchcraft and Magic. Emma Wilby. Sussex Academic Press. 2006

Cunningham's Encyclopedia of Magical Herbs. Scott Cunningham. Llewellyn Publications. 1985.

Death: A History of Man's Obsessions and Fears. Robert Wilkens. Barnes and Noble. 1990.

The Deities Are Many: A Polytheistic Theology. Jordan Paper. State University of New York Press. 2005.

The Dreamer's Book of the Dead. Robert Moss. Destiny Books. 2005.

The Egyptian Book of the Dead: The Book of Going Forth By Day. Translated by Dr. Raymond Faulkner. Chronical Books. 1994.

Egyptian Mythology: A Guide To The Gods, Goddesses, and Traditions of Ancient Egypt. Geraldine Pinch. Oxford University Press. 2002.

The Element Encyclopedia of 5000 Spells. Judika Illes. Element. 2004.

Eleusinian Mysteries and Rites. Doudley Wright. The Theosophical Publishing House.

The Essence of Shinto: Japan's Spiritual Heart. Motohisa Yamaksage. Kodansha International. 2006.

The Exorcist Handbook. Josephine McCarthy. Golem Media. 2010.

The Faery Teachings. Orion Foxwood. R.J. Steward Books. 2007.

Forbidden Rites: A Necromancer's Manual of the Fifteenth Century. Richard Kieckhefer. The Pennsylvania State University Press. 1998.

From Artemis to Diana: The Goddess of Man and Beast. 12 ACTA Hyperborea. Edited by Tobias Fischer-Hansen and Birte Poulsen. Museum Tusculanum Press. 2009.

From Distant Days: Myths, Tales, and Poetry of Ancient Mesopotamia. Benjamin R. Foster. CDL Press. 1995.

Gods, Demons, and Symbols of Ancient Mesopotamia. Jack Black and Anthony Green. University of Texas Press. 1992.

God Is Red. Vine Deloria Jr. Fulcrum Publishing. 1973.

The Gods of the Egyptians: Studies in Egyptian Mythology. E.A. Wallis Budge. Dover Publications. 1969.

The Goetia: The Lesser Key of Solomon the King. Translated by Samuel Liddell MacGregor Mathers. Samuel Weiser, Inc. 1995.

The Grail Legend. Emma Jung and Marie-Louise von Franz. Sigo Press. 1986.

Greek and Roman Necromancy. Daniel Ogden. Princeton University Press. 2001.

Greek and Roman Mythology. Thomas Bulfinch. Penguin Books. 1979.

Hecate's Fountain. Kenneth Grant. Skoob Books Publishing. 1992.

Heimskringla or The Lives of the Norse Kings. Snorri Sturluson. Dover Publications. 1990.

Hoodoo Herb and Root Magic: A Materia Magica of African-American Conjure. Catherine Yronwode. Lucky Mojo Curio Company. 2002.

Indian Mythology: Tales, Rituals, and Symbols from the Heart of the Subcontinent. Devdutt Pattanaik. Inner Traditions International. 2003.

Jotunbok: Working With The Giants of the Northern Tradition. Raven Kaldera. Asphodel Press. 2006.

Julian of Norwich: Revelations of Divine Love. Translated into modern English by Clifton Wolters. Penguin Books. 1966.

The Lost Secret of Death. Peter Novak. Hampton Roads Publishing. 2003.

Low Magick. Lon Milo Duquette. Llewellyn. 2010.

Magic and Superstition In Europe: A Concise History From Antiquity To The Present. Michael D. Bailey. Rowman and Littlefield Publishers, INC. 2007

Magical Use of Thought Forms: A Proven System of Mental and Spiritual Empowerment. Dolores Ashcraft-Nowicki and J.H. Brennan. Llewellyn Publications. 2002.

Masks of Misrule. Nigel Jackson. Capall Bann Publishing. 1996.

The Master Book of Herbalism. Paul Beyerl. Phoenix Publishing Co. 1984.

Modern Magick: Twelve Lessons in the High Magickal Arts. Donald Michael Kraig. Llewellyn Publications. 1988.

The Mythic Path. David Feinstein, Ph.D. and Stanley Krippner, Ph.D. Tarcher/Putnam Books. 1997.

The Myth of Isis and Osiris. Jules Cashford. Barefoot Books. 1993.

Netherworld. Robert Temple. Century Publications. 2002.

The Nightbattles: Witchcraft and Agrarian Cults in the Sixteenth and Seventeenth Centuries. Carlo Ginzburg. Translated by John and Ann Tedeschi. Penguin Books. 1983.

Norse Mythology: The Guide To The Gods, Heroes, Rituals, and Beliefs. John Lindow. Oxford University Press. 2001.

The Norse Myths. Kevin Crossley-Holland. Pantheon Books. 1980.

Osiris and the Egyptian Resurrection. E.A. Wallis Budge. Dover Publications. 1973.

Our Name Is Melancholy: The Complete Books of Azrael. Leilah Wendell. West Gate Press. 1992.

The Pathwalker's Guide To The Nine Worlds. Raven Kaldera. Asphodel Press. 2006.

Popol Vuh. Translated by Dennis Tedlock. Touchstone. Simon and Schuster Publishing. 1985, 1996.

The Practice of Dream Healing: Bringing Ancient Greek Mysteries Into Modern Practice. Edward Tick, Ph.D. Quest Books. 2001.

The Prose Edda. Snorri Sturluson. Translated by Jesse L. Byock. Penguin Press. 2005.

The Poetic Edda. Translated by Lee M. Hollander. University of Texas Press, Austin. 1962.

The Robert Cochrane Letters: An Insight into Modern Traditional Witchcraft. Robert Cochrane with Evan John Jones. Capall Bann. 2002.

The Roebuck In The Thicket: An Anthology of the Robert Cochrane Witchcraft Tradition. Evan John Jones and Robert Cochrane. 2001.

The Sacred Pipe: Black Elk's Account of the Seven Rites of the Oglala Sioux. Oklahoma Press. 1953.

The Secret Commonwealth of Elves, Fauns and Fairies. Robert Kirk. Dover Publications, Inc. 2008.

The Shaman's Secret: The Lost Resurrection Teachings of the Ancient Maya. Douglas Gillette, M.A., M. Div. Bantam Books. 1997.

The Spiritual Universe: The Existence of the Soul. Fred Alan Wolf, Ph.D. Simon and Schuster. 1996.

Summoning Spirits: The Art of Magical Evocation. Konstantinos. Llewellyn Publications. 1996.

Temple of the Cosmos: The Ancient Egyptian Experience of the Sacred. Jeremy Naydler. Inner Traditions International. 1996.

The Tibetan Book of the Dead: The Great Book of Natural Liberation Through Understanding In The Between. Translated by Robert A.F. Thurman. Bantam Books. 1994.

Treading the Mill: Practical Craft Working in Modern Traditional Witchcraft. Nigel G. Pearson. Capall Bann Publishing. 2007.

Understanding In The Between. Translated by Robert A.F. Thurman. Bantam Books. 1994.

The Underworld Initiation: A Journey Towards Psychic Transformation. R. J. Stewart. Mercury Publishing Inc. 1990.

Walking The Twilight Path: A Gothic Book of the Dead. Michelle Belanger. Llewellyn Publications. 2008.

Wightridden: Paths of Northern-Tradition Shamanism. Raven Kaldera. Asphodel Press. 2007.

Wyrdwalkers: Techniques of Norther-Traditions Shamanism. Raven Kaldera. Asphodel Press. 2006.

Index

A

Aesculapius 65
African 27, 118, 187, 211
Afterlife 7, 10, 11, 25, 43, 45, 48, 53, 82, 86, 104, 136, 139, 143, 168
Altar 9, 10, 47, 63, 74, 76, 82, 84, 85, 86, 87, 88, 89, 90, 92, 93, 94, 95, 96, 101, 105, 106, 114, 115, 116, 117, 118, 119, 184, 192, 197, 199
Ammit 44
Ammonia 197
Ancestral Teacher 11, 107, 108, 109, 112
Angel 11, 24, 29, 30, 31, 33, 34, 99, 157
  of Death 28, 29, 30, 31, 32, 34, 205
Anger 39, 94
Annwn 10, 139
Anubis 58
Apollo 52, 164, 179
Ariel 33, 34, 202, 204
Artemis 178, 210
Asclepius 163, 164, 165, 179
Astral 11, 12, 13, 17, 18, 20, 21, 36, 38, 39, 40, 58, 59, 90, 95, 96, 97, 104, 109, 126, 134, 135, 141, 146, 155, 173, 175, 180, 186, 197
Astral body 11, 12, 17, 39, 40, 58, 59, 104, 109, 141
Astral projection 12, 13
Aura 20, 73
Ayurvedic Medicine 176
Azrael 29, 30, 31, 32, 33, 34, 212

B

Ba 58
Baia 82
Baldur 121, 152
Beeswax 89, 147
Bible 43
Blood 8, 9, 62, 63, 83, 104, 109, 111, 112, 117, 133, 134, 138, 140, 141, 146, 148, 149, 176, 177, 178, 179, 180, 181, 182, 183, 184, 185, 186, 187, 188, 189, 190, 207
  magick 176, 187
Bloodlines 8, 137
Body of light 12
Bones 84, 123, 133, 147, 168, 169, 172, 174, 175, 176, 179, 190, 198, 207
Brahma 34, 55
Buddhism 41, 50
Burial mounds 124

C

Celtic 27, 118, 125, 132, 169, 171, 178, 209
Cemeteries 82, 126, 127, 128, 130, 133, 206
Cernunnos 101
Chakras 36, 37
Charms 54, 59, 121, 198
Charon 63, 128, 139, 164
Chi 176
Chicago 130
Christian 28, 29, 43, 44, 45, 48, 71, 122, 137, 142, 151, 179, 181, 189
Chthonic deities 11
Clairvoyants 97
Corpse 27, 58, 126, 147, 160, 161, 162, 164, 169, 175
Cosmic 10, 28, 35, 45, 46, 51,

161
Coyote 22
Cremated 38
Crypt 170
Cunning Man 137
Cupid 31
Curse 155, 170, 183, 187

D
Dark Elves 108
Dark Gods 160
Dead
  Lord of 150
  Temple of the 59, 82, 205
Death
  Goddess of 138, 139
  rites 7
Deathwalker 48
Decay 24, 27, 33, 39, 53, 57, 125, 128
Demeter 64, 66, 67, 69, 150
Demons 11, 24, 31, 40, 49, 56, 63, 66, 67, 122, 142, 148, 157, 177, 181, 187, 190, 191, 195
Dharma 44
Diana 139, 163, 164, 165, 178, 210
Divination 27, 56, 86, 87, 108, 116, 119, 122, 123, 125, 143, 152, 162, 169, 171, 206
DNA 8, 9, 110, 111, 112, 124, 176, 180, 183, 186, 189
Doll 147
Dreams 100, 121, 132
Drum 13, 73, 75, 76, 202
Duat 10, 58, 59, 179
Dunlop, Bessie 56
Dwarves 108

E
eclipse
  Solar 70
Egypt 10, 44, 55, 57, 58, 59, 130, 142, 149, 158, 205, 209, 210, 212, 213
Eleusinian Mysteries 65, 205, 210
Elysium 139
Etheric 38, 39
Eulogy 49, 50, 51
Europe 55, 156, 169, 211
Eurydice 52, 53

F
Faerie Mounds 124
Fate 140, 141
Fear 24, 26, 27, 28, 29, 30, 31, 33, 43, 48, 49, 61, 72, 137, 151, 175, 193, 194, 205
Fellowship of the Phoenix 75
Freya 45, 167, 182
Freyr 55, 167
Full moon 125, 199
Fumigation 146, 197
Funeral 40, 47, 49, 50, 51, 57

G
Gabriel 33, 34, 202
Gatekeeper 127, 129, 131, 149, 150
Genesis 178
Ghost Dance 69, 70, 71, 72, 205
Goddess of Death 139, 140, 141, 142
Gods 7, 8, 10, 11, 13, 21, 24, 28, 31, 35, 42, 44, 46, 54, 55, 57, 59, 60, 61, 65, 66, 67, 73, 81, 90, 97, 98, 100, 101, 102, 103, 107, 113, 114, 116, 117, 119, 129, 130, 132, 144, 146, 148, 150, 154, 155, 156, 158, 160, 164, 165, 168, 171, 178, 179, 181, 182, 183, 186, 189, 198, 199, 203, 204, 206
Goetia 56, 210
Graves 27, 123, 127, 133
Gravestone 135, 175

Greco-Roman 52, 59, 60, 101, 134, 150, 163, 179, 187, 195
Greeks 10, 27, 56, 59, 66, 142, 149, 205
Grimoires 151, 155, 157, 161, 190
Guardian 99, 130, 131, 132
Gwyn Ap Nudd 101

H
Hades 10, 17, 27, 52, 59, 60, 61, 63, 64, 65, 66, 67, 68, 149, 150, 154, 187, 205
Halloween 29, 83
Hallucinogens 62
Healing 7, 8, 10, 11, 30, 54, 56, 65, 77, 86, 96, 97, 98, 106, 107, 113, 116, 118, 135, 137, 142, 153, 155, 156, 157, 163, 164, 166, 177, 179, 181, 196, 206, 207
Heaven 23, 29, 52, 86, 155, 157
Hecate 101, 139, 149, 150, 154, 211
Hedge Witch 137
Hel 10, 17, 121, 139, 154, 167
Helheim 45, 121
Hell 23, 29, 43, 45, 48, 86, 155, 157
Hella 101
Herbs 62, 146, 167, 195, 198
Hermes 65, 101
Hidden Company 136, 137, 138, 139, 140, 142
High Priestess 60
Hindu 34, 35, 44, 118
Holy Medicine People 98
Horus 58, 158, 159
Hyndla 182

I
Illness 30
Inanna 161
Incense 58, 63, 74, 148, 188, 197, 199
Indigenous 11, 54, 82, 97, 98, 151, 187
Isis 58, 158, 159, 161, 211
Islamic 28

J
Jesus 43, 161, 179
Jewish 28, 29, 31, 118
Judeo-Christian 24, 31, 43, 156, 177
Judgment 43, 44, 45
Julian 43, 211

K
Karma 38, 41, 42, 44, 81, 83, 110, 113, 114

L
Lakota 69, 70, 72, 97, 205
Lesser Banishing Ritual of the Pentagram 118, 143, 201, 202, 204
Life force 36, 40, 54, 63, 104, 106, 148, 176, 177, 184, 186, 189, 191
lineage
   Magical 138

M
Maat 44, 59, 159
Magical lineage 8, 9, 114
Massacre at Wounded Knee 72
Mausoleums 82, 129, 130, 131, 206
Maya 178, 179, 188, 212
Medicine 22, 107, 137
Memories 17, 40, 46, 48, 107, 173
Mercury 101, 213
Michael 33, 34, 143, 202, 209, 211
Middleworld 15, 17, 21, 53, 63, 65, 150, 152, 159, 196
Midworld 8, 11, 15, 16, 18, 109
Mimirs 167
Mirrors 201
Mother Earth 22, 33, 34

Mrityu 34
Music 13, 14, 16, 33, 52, 73, 74, 76

N
Native American 22, 54, 69, 70, 71, 98, 118, 206
Native spirituality 71
Nature spirits 81, 100, 146, 148, 154, 156
Necromancy 27, 56, 58, 100, 121, 122, 123, 125, 132, 133, 134, 135, 147, 150, 151, 156, 157, 159, 162, 168, 169, 175, 186, 190, 205, 211
Necropolis 131
Nordic 10, 45, 55, 57, 125, 187
Northern European 126, 130

O
Odin 45, 55, 57, 121, 152, 161, 167, 182
Offering 61, 62, 63, 88, 90, 101, 102, 134, 135, 149, 177
Olympus 65
Oracle 27, 56, 60, 132, 142, 171, 176
Orpheus 52, 53
Osiris 55, 58, 59, 101, 161, 179, 209, 211, 212
Otherworld 11, 38, 102, 157, 207
Ottar 182

P
Palestine 178
Persephone 52, 61, 62, 63, 64, 66, 67, 68, 101, 149, 150, 154
Physical plane 12, 17, 23, 28, 35, 39, 40, 50, 59, 90, 91, 99, 100, 101, 104, 115, 133, 138, 141, 142, 147, 152, 157, 169, 184, 186, 191, 203, 204
Pine Ridge 72
Poppet 147
Prana 176
Prophecy 56, 57, 137, 162
Psychic 93, 95, 126, 165, 173, 194
Psychopomp 29

R
Re-animation 147, 159, 164
Realm of the Dead 29, 61, 121, 123, 124, 170, 208
Rebirth 7, 29, 35, 44, 138, 139, 205
Reid, Tom 57
Reincarnation 44, 55
Ring 194
River of Forgetfulness 61
River Styx 63
Romans 27, 59, 139, 148, 149, 150, 178, 205
Rose 138, 163
  Castle 138, 139, 140, 141
Runes 87, 116, 143, 167, 187, 193

S
Sabbat 192
Sacrifice 59, 61, 63, 66, 95, 161, 177, 178, 190
Samhain 75, 83, 125
Shadow
  dance 75
  lands 11
Shamanic 122, 187
  drumming 13, 14, 16
  journeying 13
  worlds 12, 207
Shapeshifters 48, 137
Skeleton 147, 174
Skull 27, 36, 84, 121, 140, 141, 147, 162, 168, 169, 170, 171, 172, 207
Solstice
  Winter 125
Soul 7, 11, 24, 27, 29, 31, 40, 44, 57, 77, 123, 138, 169,

171, 172, 173, 179, 189
retrieval 173
Spells 12, 54, 59, 116, 128, 162, 164, 165, 167, 196
Spirit
  body 40
Spirit Animal 18, 19, 20, 112
Spirit guides 11, 80, 81, 98, 104, 117
Spiritual evolution 11, 31, 90, 93, 99, 118, 207
Sun 52, 58, 70, 79, 125, 126, 139, 158, 161, 164, 194, 196
  dance 97
Svartalfheim 108
Sybil 60, 62, 63, 64

T
Talisman 199
Tarot 87, 116, 143
Tartarus 11, 63, 66
Temple 50, 60, 61, 62, 66, 82, 127, 131, 140, 144, 145, 150, 178, 191, 192, 197, 203, 204
Thor 55, 182
Titans 10
Traditional Chinese Medicine 176
Traditional Witchcraft 136, 139, 212, 213
Transformation 18, 21, 41, 45, 55, 93, 98

Trickster spirits 106, 148

U
Underworld Guide 18, 20, 21
Unfinished business 39, 98, 110, 153
Upperworld 8, 11, 45, 57, 159, 207

V
Valhalla 45, 139
Vampire 26, 40, 149
Veil 8, 48, 71, 75, 105
Volva 57

W
Wards 193
Welsh 10, 139
Wicca 136
Wilson, Jack 69, 70, 71, 72
Witchblood 180, 181
Witchs broom 143, 192
World Tree 15, 16, 17, 18, 20, 108, 161

Y
Yahweh 33, 34
Yama 35
Yami 35
Yule 125

Z
Zeus 10, 53, 65, 67, 179